Betty Crocker

tiny bites

Houghton Mifflin Harcourt
Boston • New York • 2014

GENERAL MILLS

Food Content and Relationship Marketing Director: Geoff Johnson

Food Content Marketing Manager: Heather Reid Liebo

Senior Editor: Grace Wells

Kitchen Manager: Ann Stuart

Food Editor: Kristen Olson

Recipe Development and Testing: Betty Crocker Kitchens

Photography: General Mills Photography Studios and Image Library

HOUGHTON MIFFLIN HARCOURT

Publisher: Natalie Chapman

Editorial Director: Cindy Kitchel

Executive Editor: Anne Ficklen

Senior Editor: Adam Kowit

Editorial Associate: Molly Aronica

Managing Editor: Marina Padakis

Production Editors: Helen Seachrist and Jamie Selzer

Cover Design: Tai Blanche

Interior Design and Layout: Tai Blanche

Production Coordinator: Kimberly Kiefer

The Betty Crocker Kitchens seal guarantees success in your kitchen. Every recipe has been tested in America's Most Trusted Kitchens™ to meet our high standards of reliability, easy preparation and great taste.

FIND MORE GREAT IDEAS AT
Betty Crocker.com

This book is printed on acid-free paper. ∞

www.hmhco.com

Library of Congress Cataloging-in-Publication Data:

Crocker, Betty.

Betty Crocker tiny bites.

pages cm

Includes index.

ISBN 978-0-544-33444-1 (trade paper : acid-free paper)

ISBN 978-0-544-33260-7 (ebk)

1. Snack foods. 2. Appetizers. I. Title. II. Title: Tiny bites.

TX740.C684 2014

642—dc23

2014016520

Manufactured in the United States of America

DOC 10 9 8 7 6 5 4 3 2 1

Cover photos: Peach and Cheesy Caprese Bites (page 116), Mini Corn Cakes (page 84), Stout French Silk Cookie Cups (page 160), Tequila Sunrise Cake Pops (page 142) Black Bean Sliders (page 70), Dark Chocolate–Raspberry Trifle Shooters (page 124), Mini Pancake-Avocado Stacks (page 44)

Dear Friends,

What could be more charming than a tray of your favorite foods served in cute, bite-size portions? Maybe you're in the mood to serve something special but don't want a full meal? Or it's a Sunday morning and you want variety for a breakfast buffet. It could also be as simple as a Saturday evening when everyone wants just a little of this or a little of that. What you are craving are small versions of foods that you love, and this book is chock-full of fun, fanciful ideas.

Turning the pages will enchant and inspire, so go ahead and start browsing—you're sure to find something perfect for whatever occasion you're planning. And, there's a full-color photo of each recipe to help make it easy to choose. It's really up to you whether you serve one, two or a few of these delectable recipes.

Recipes like Dark Chocolate–Raspberry Trifle Shooters (page 124), Spiced Sweet Potato–Turkey Sliders (page 68) and Peach and Cheesy Caprese Bites (page 116) are just the start of the fun. Everyone enjoys picking from platters of whimsical small foods, whether it's a mini meal, a petite bread or a darling dessert—and with these exquisite morsels, there's always room for more!

So let *Betty Crocker Tiny Bites* decorate the day—bet you can't make just one!

Delightfully,
Betty Crocker

contents

Think Small!

The beauty of tiny bites is in their versatility—they're fun, fanciful and ideal for any occasion. You can make up one recipe for a snack or dessert, several to make a mini meal or petite breakfast or go all out for a cocktail party. It's all up to you.

Small Equipment

For many of the recipes, we use special equipment that works well for creating tiny bites. You may have some items on hand, but here's a list of our favorites. Look for them all at large department or specialty stores or online.

- Miniature muffin pans
- Regular muffin pans
- Small or miniature loaf pans
- Miniature tart pans
- Small custard cups
- Shot glasses in a variety of shapes and sizes
- Small or miniature martini glasses
- Miniature paper candy cups
- Decorative toothpicks
- Decorative skewers
- Miniature spoons

Mini Party Bites Tips!

Here are some tips to help with any kind of party, from small and casual to large and fancy.

It's in the Planning

Your theme makes the atmosphere—decide this based on time of year, who will attend and what the occasion is that you are planning for.

- Create your mini-bites menu with an eye toward types of foods, flavors and textures. Allow for 2 or 3 pieces or bites for each food you choose. Many recipes can be easily doubled or tripled for larger gatherings with just a few simple calculations. If you want to double a muffin or other baked good, make 2 batches as these foods can be tricky to multiply.

- Map out a timeline of what you want to serve, how many guests will attend, where you will serve, etc.

- If you are making several recipes, try to make one or two that you can do ahead. Many chilled items can be made ahead of time and kept in the refrigerator. Also, prepping parts of a recipe ahead of time and storing each ingredient separately makes last-minute assembly faster.

- It's okay to pick up a few things at the deli! Serve purchased olives, pickles and other small foods in individual containers like shot glasses, tiny plates or small bowls—use your imagination and have fun with the presentation!

Food Choices

- Try to mix hot and cold appetizers, things on a stick, shot-glass foods and finger foods—you get the idea. Also, unless you are serving a mini-dessert buffet, it's nice to mix sweet and savory foods.

- Choose different colored foods and serve them on a variety of decorative plates—keeping your theme in mind.

- Serve a variety of food types—one person may gravitate toward the healthier options, while another looks for heartier bites.

Temperature Matters

Serve hot items like sliders, tarts and hand pies as quickly as possible after assembling. Cover with foil if necessary for a few minutes. Keep extra-hot bites in the oven at a very low temperature so they are ready to serve when you need them.

Keep cold foods in the refrigerator until serving time and refill platters as needed. For foods that need to stay chilled, set the serving bowl or plate into a bowl filled with ice.

The Buffet Table

Buffets are a great option for any gathering, but this serving style is especially nice for informal get-togethers. So whether you are serving a petite breakfast buffet, a mini dessert sampler or a casual tiny-food dinner occasion, here are some tips to help with your buffet.

- Set up the buffet on a center island, dining table, sideboard or counter. Be sure there is room for guests to move around the serving area. For a larger gathering, set up several areas with different bites so guests can browse and graze at a leisurely pace.

- Start with the plates and foods, then place the eating utensils and napkins at the end. Add some small trays (available at craft or specialty stores) for guests to gather the tiny bites easily. Beverages can be at the end of the area or on another table or surface and can also be placed on the trays.

- Make cutlery bundles for easy handling—wrap with cloth or paper napkins.

Tiny Menus

Although this whimsical book is made up of foods that are all small, it's fun to combine and create menus with the recipes. Think of your occasion, then browse the book for recipes that suit the time of day and theme. Our goal is to inspire, so here are a few ideas to start with—use your imagination to substitute other recipes as they fit into your own occasion. Be sure to think miniature when planning and choose small plates, miniature spoons for coffee or tea, cocktail forks and petite colorful napkins to help create the atmosphere!

Mini Breakfast to Share

Sweet Potato Pie Mini Cinnamon Rolls, pages 20–21

Fresh berries

Bacon, Kale and Egg Cups, page 80

Doughnut Bites with Spicy Hot Chocolate, page 16

* * * * *

Appetizer Bites Anytime

Fire-Roasted Crab Shooters, page 102

Or

Cold cocktail shrimp with cocktail sauce

Cheesy Fig Bites, page 112

Spiced Sweet Potato–Turkey Sliders, page 68

Pomegranate–Tequila Sunrise Jelly Shots, page 134

Chocolate truffles or other chocolates

* * * * *

Tea Time with Small Plates

Impossibly Easy Brussels Sprouts Mini Pies, page 82

Peach and Cheesy Caprese Bites, page 116

Or

Fruit Salsa Crostini, page 48

Chocolate-Dipped Olive Sablés, page 170

Hot tea

Lemon wedges, honey, milk

* * * * *

Fun Lunch for a Bunch

Black Bean Sliders, page 70

Or

Mini Greek Burgers, page 64

Potato Salad Bites, page 114

Veggie Strips with Sriracha Hummus, page 118

Stout French Silk Cookie Cups, page 160

* * * * *

Wedding Reception Buffet Sampler

Fresh fruit bowl

Platter of olives and sliced sausage with small breads and crackers

California Sushi Canapés, page 104

Fire-Roasted Crab Shooters, page 102

Mini Cheese Balls (French, Korean, Mexican and/or Indian), pages 106–109

Cookies and Cream Mini Cheesecakes, page 186

Cake and Ice Cream Shots, page 132

Champagne

* * * * *

Saturday Night Snacks on the Deck

Spicy Mini Dogs, page 96

BLT Crostini, page 50

Miniature dill pickles

Mini Beer-Pimiento-Cheese Muffins, page 40

Fresh vegetable platter

Chipotle Devil's Food Mini Cupcakes, pages 180–181

Beer and wine

* * * * *

petite breads

From adorable doughnut holes to delectable mini pancakes, these bite-size breads will meet all your sweet and savory needs!

maple-glazed bacon drop doughnuts

PREP TIME: **1 Hour 20 Minutes** | START TO FINISH: **1 Hour 20 Minutes** | **24 doughnuts**

DOUGHNUTS

Vegetable oil, for deep frying

1	egg
½	cup milk
2	tablespoons butter, melted
1½	cups all-purpose flour
¼	cup packed brown sugar
2	teaspoons baking powder
½	teaspoon salt
½	teaspoon ground cinnamon
6	slices maple-flavored bacon, crisply cooked, crumbled

MAPLE GLAZE

3	cups powdered sugar
⅓	cup water
⅓	cup maple-flavored syrup

1 In deep fryer or 3-quart saucepan, heat 2 inches oil to 350°F.

2 Meanwhile, in large bowl, beat egg, milk and butter with fork. Stir in flour, brown sugar, baking powder, salt, cinnamon and bacon.

3 Carefully drop dough by heaping tablespoons, 6 balls at a time, into hot oil. Fry doughnut balls 30 seconds to 1 minute on each side, or until golden brown. Remove from oil with slotted spoon; drain on paper towels until cooled, about 20 minutes.

4 In medium bowl, mix powdered sugar and water until smooth; stir in maple-flavored syrup. Add additional water, 1 teaspoon at a time, until thick glazing consistency. Dip cool doughnut balls into glaze; let excess drip off. (If glaze disappears while drying, glaze may be too thin. Try dipping balls again, or thicken up glaze by adding a small amount of powdered sugar.) Place glazed doughnut balls on cooling rack; let stand until glaze is set, about 10 minutes.

1 Doughnut: Calories 180; Total Fat 7g (Saturated Fat 1.5g, Trans Fat 0g); Cholesterol 15mg; Sodium 150mg; Total Carbohydrate 27g (Dietary Fiber 0g); Protein 2g **Exchanges:** ½ Starch, 1½ Other Carbohydrate, 1½ Fat **Carbohydrate Choices:** 2

tidbits

Instead of heaping tablespoons of dough, use a #60 or #70 ice cream scoop (1¼ inches in diameter) to spoon the dough into the oil.

Cook bacon quickly in the microwave. Place the slices on a microwavable plate lined with paper towels; cover with a paper towel. Microwave on High 3 to 5 minutes or until crisp.

doughnut bites with spicy hot chocolate

PREP TIME: 1 Hour | **START TO FINISH: 1 Hour** | **24 servings**

DOUGHNUTS

Vegetable oil, for deep frying

1/3 cup granulated sugar

1 teaspoon ground cinnamon

1/8 teaspoon ground red pepper (cayenne)

1 cup Original Bisquick™ mix

2 tablespoons granulated sugar

3 tablespoons milk

1 tablespoon butter, melted

1 egg yolk

HOT CHOCOLATE

1 quart (4 cups) whole milk or half-and-half

1½ cups water

3/4 cup packed brown sugar

2 tablespoons instant espresso coffee powder or granules

1/8 teaspoon ground red pepper (cayenne) or chili powder

2 teaspoons vanilla

2 (2- to 3-inch) cinnamon sticks

6 oz bittersweet baking chocolate, chopped

1 In deep fryer or 2-quart saucepan, heat 2 inches oil to 375°F. In small bowl, mix 1/3 cup granulated sugar, the cinnamon and 1/8 teaspoon ground red pepper; set aside.

2 In medium bowl, mix Bisquick mix, 2 tablespoons sugar, the milk, butter and egg yolk until smooth. Using small cookie scoop sprayed generously with cooking spray, shape dough into 24 (1-inch) balls. Carefully drop balls, 5 or 6 at a time, into hot oil. Fry 1 to 2 minutes, turning halfway through frying, until golden brown on all sides. Remove from oil with slotted spoon; drain on paper towels briefly. Roll in spiced sugar mixture.

3 In 3-quart saucepan, mix all hot chocolate ingredients except chocolate. Cover; cook over medium-low heat about 30 minutes, stirring occasionally, just until simmering (do not boil).

4 Remove saucepan from heat; remove cinnamon sticks. With whisk, stir in chocolate. Pour hot chocolate into mugs or cups. Garnish each serving as desired.

1 Serving: Calories 180; Total Fat 10g (Saturated Fat 4g, Trans Fat 0g); Cholesterol 15mg; Sodium 90mg; Total Carbohydrate 18g (Dietary Fiber 1g); Protein 2g **Exchanges:** ½ Starch, ½ Other Carbohydrate, 2 Fat **Carbohydrate Choices:** 1

tidbit

Hot chocolate is best when frothy. To achieve this effect, vigorously stir the hot chocolate with a whisk until very frothy just before pouring into mugs to serve. If you like, garnish with frozen whipped topping, additional ground red pepper and cinnamon sticks.

snickerdoodle mini doughnuts

PREP TIME: 45 Minutes | **START TO FINISH:** 1 Hour 45 Minutes | **26 mini doughnuts**

DOUGHNUTS

⅓ cup sugar

¼ cup butter, melted

2 eggs

⅓ cup milk

3 tablespoons sour cream

1 teaspoon vanilla

2 cups all-purpose flour

1½ teaspoons ground cinnamon

1 teaspoon cream of tartar

1 teaspoon baking powder

TOPPING

¾ cup sugar

3 tablespoons ground cinnamon

6 tablespoons butter, melted

tidbits

Refrigerating the dough makes it easier to roll, but extra flour is still needed to keep the dough from sticking to the counter and rolling pin. Shake off any excess flour before placing the dough rounds on the cookie sheet.

Cream of tartar adds the signature sweet-sour "snickerdoodle" taste to these doughnuts, distinguishing them from the regular cinnamon-sugar variety.

1 In medium bowl, mix ⅓ cup sugar, ¼ cup butter and the eggs until smooth. Stir in milk, sour cream and vanilla with whisk. Stir in flour, 1½ teaspoons cinnamon, the cream of tartar and baking powder just until moistened.

2 Grease medium bowl with shortening. Place dough in bowl. Cover bowl with plastic wrap; refrigerate 1 hour.

3 Heat oven to 450°F. Line 2 cookie sheets with cooking parchment paper. Place dough on surface generously sprinkled with flour. Roll dough in flour to coat. With floured rolling pin, roll dough to ½-inch thickness. Cut dough with floured 1¾-inch round cutter. Place dough rounds on cookie sheets about 1 inch apart. Cut out centers using floured ¾-inch round cutter. Reroll scraps to cut additional doughnuts.

4 Bake 8 to 10 minutes or until edges just turn light golden brown. Immediately transfer from cookie sheet to cooling rack. Cool 3 minutes.

5 In small bowl, stir together ¾ cup sugar and 3 tablespoons cinnamon. Place 6 tablespoons melted butter in another small bowl. Quickly dip both sides of each warm doughnut into butter; let excess drip off. Using spoon, roll each doughnut in cinnamon-sugar mixture to coat. Return doughnuts to cooling rack. Serve warm.

1 Mini Doughnut: Calories 120; Total Fat 5g (Saturated Fat 3g, Trans Fat 0g); Cholesterol 30mg; Sodium 60mg; Total Carbohydrate 17g (Dietary Fiber 1g); Protein 1g **Exchanges:** ½ Starch, ½ Other Carbohydrate, 1 Fat **Carbohydrate Choices:** 1

sweet potato pie
mini cinnamon rolls

PREP TIME: 40 Minutes | **START TO FINISH: 3 Hours** | **24 mini rolls**

ROLLS

1½	to 1¾ cups all-purpose or bread flour
2	tablespoons granulated sugar
½	teaspoon salt
¼	teaspoon ground cinnamon
1¼	teaspoons fast-acting dry yeast
¼	cup very warm milk (120°F to 130°F)
⅓	cup mashed cooked sweet potato, cooled
3	tablespoons butter, softened
1	egg yolk

FILLING

2	tablespoons butter, softened
2	tablespoons packed brown sugar
2	teaspoons ground cinnamon
½	teaspoon ground ginger
½	teaspoon ground nutmeg
¼	teaspoon ground cardamom
⅛	teaspoon ground cloves

GLAZE

2	tablespoons butter, melted
1	tablespoon plus 1 to 2 teaspoons milk
1	cup powdered sugar

1 In large bowl, mix 1 cup of the flour, the granulated sugar, salt, ¼ teaspoon cinnamon and the yeast. Add warm milk, sweet potato, 3 tablespoons butter and the egg yolk. Beat with electric mixer on low speed 1 minute, scraping bowl frequently. Beat on medium speed 1 minute, scraping bowl frequently. Stir in enough remaining flour, ¼ cup at a time, to make dough easy to handle.

2 Place dough on lightly floured surface. Knead 3 to 5 minutes or until dough is smooth and springy. Grease medium bowl with shortening. Place dough in bowl, turning dough to grease all sides. Cover bowl loosely with plastic wrap sprayed with cooking spray; let rise in warm place about 1 hour 15 minutes or until dough has doubled in size. Dough is ready if indentation remains when touched.

3 In small bowl, mix 1 tablespoon of the butter and the remaining filling ingredients; set aside.

4 Grease bottoms and sides of 24 mini muffin cups with shortening, or spray with cooking spray. Gently push fist into dough to deflate. On lightly floured surface, flatten dough with hands or rolling pin into 12x9-inch rectangle. Cut dough in half forming 2 (9x6-inch) rectangles. Spread rectangles with remaining 1 tablespoon butter; sprinkle with filling, covering entire surface. Roll rectangle up tightly, beginning at 9-inch side. Pinch edge of dough into roll to seal. Stretch and shape until even. Cut each roll into 12 (¾-inch) slices with dental floss or sharp serrated knife.

5 Place each slice in muffin cup, cut side up. Cover loosely with plastic wrap sprayed with cooking spray; let rise in warm place 30 minutes.

6 Heat oven to 350°F. Bake 10 to 12 minutes or until light golden brown. Immediately transfer from pans to cooling rack.

7 Meanwhile, in small bowl, stir 2 tablespoons melted butter, 1 tablespoon milk and the powdered sugar. Stir in additional milk, 1 teaspoon at a time, until glaze is smooth and consistency of thick syrup. Drizzle over rolls. Serve warm.

1 Mini Roll: Calories 100; Total Fat 3.5g (Saturated Fat 2.5g, Trans Fat 0g); Cholesterol 20mg; Sodium 75mg; Total Carbohydrate 14g (Dietary Fiber 0g); Protein 1g **Exchanges:** ½ Starch, ½ Other Carbohydrate, ½ Fat **Carbohydrate Choices:** 1

tidbits

To easily cook the sweet potato, pierce with a fork and place on a paper towel in the microwave. Microwave on High 5 to 7 minutes or until tender. Cool until easy enough to handle. Slit potato skin and peel away from flesh. Mash flesh with fork and let cool to room temperature.

mini cinnamon bun treats

PREP TIME: **25 Minutes** | START TO FINISH: **1 Hour 10 Minutes** | **16 mini buns**

⅓ cup packed brown sugar

3 teaspoons pumpkin pie spice

1 can (8-oz) refrigerated seamless dough sheet

¼ cup butter, softened

16 paper lollipop sticks

1 oz cream cheese (from 3-oz package), softened

1 tablespoon butter, softened

¼ cup powdered sugar

¼ teaspoon vanilla

3 teaspoons milk

1 Heat oven to 350°F. Spray 16 mini muffin cups with cooking spray. In small bowl, mix brown sugar and pumpkin pie spice.

2 Unroll dough sheet on lightly floured surface. Spread with ¼ cup butter; sprinkle with brown sugar mixture, pressing lightly. Starting with long side, roll dough up tightly. Cut into 16 (¾-inch) slices. Place slices, cut side down, in muffin cups.

3 Bake 13 to 15 minutes or until golden brown. Immediately remove buns from pans; insert lollipop stick into side of each bun. Cool on cooling racks 30 minutes.

4 In medium bowl, beat cream cheese and 1 tablespoon butter with electric mixer on medium speed until smooth. Gradually beat in powdered sugar and vanilla. Slowly beat in milk, 1 teaspoon at a time, until glaze is thin enough to drizzle. Spoon glaze into small resealable food-storage plastic bag; seal bag. Cut off tiny corner of bag; squeeze bag to drizzle glaze over buns. Store covered in refrigerator.

1 Mini Bun: Calories 110; Total Fat 7g (Saturated Fat 3.5g, Trans Fat 0g); Cholesterol 10mg; Sodium 150mg; Total Carbohydrate 13g (Dietary Fiber 0g); Protein 1g **Exchanges:** 1 Other Carbohydrate, 1½ Fat **Carbohydrate Choices:** 1

stir 'n scoop mini rolls

PREP TIME: 15 Minutes | **START TO FINISH:** 30 Minutes | 18 mini rolls

ROLLS

2	cups all-purpose flour
1	tablespoon sugar
2½	teaspoons baking powder
½	teaspoon salt
⅓	cup butter, softened
⅔	cup milk

TOPPING

2	tablespoons Caesar or Italian dressing
¼	teaspoon Italian seasoning
2	teaspoons grated Parmesan cheese

1 Heat oven to 400°F. Grease cookie sheet. In medium bowl, mix flour, sugar, baking powder and salt. Cut in butter, using fork, until mixture is crumbly. Stir in ⅔ cup milk until dough forms a ball and leaves side of bowl. Stir in additional milk, if necessary, 1 tablespoon at a time, until dough is soft and slightly sticky. Beat 25 strokes.

2 On cookie sheet, drop dough by rounded tablespoonfuls about 1 inch apart. In small bowl, mix dressing and seasoning. Brush over tops of rolls. Sprinkle with cheese.

3 Bake about 12 minutes or until golden brown. Serve warm.

1 Mini Roll: Calories 100; Total Fat 4.5g (Saturated Fat 2.5g, Trans Fat 0g); Cholesterol 10mg; Sodium 180mg; Total Carbohydrate 12g (Dietary Fiber 0g); Protein 2g **Exchanges:** 1 Starch, ½ Fat **Carbohydrate Choices:** 1

flavor variation

For an almond butter topping, in small bowl, mix 1½ tablespoons chopped sliced almonds, 1 tablespoon softened butter and 1 tablespoon light corn syrup. Spread over tops of unbaked rolls; sprinkle with 2 teaspoons sugar. Bake as directed.

tidbit

Get the scoop on quick cleanup! Line a cookie sheet with cooking parchment paper before dropping the dough. Simply toss the paper after baking the rolls.

mini popovers with flavored butter trio

PREP TIME: **25 Minutes** | START TO FINISH: **50 Minutes** | **32 mini popovers**

POPOVERS

- ¾ cup water
- ¼ cup butter
- 1 cup Original Bisquick mix
- 4 eggs

APRICOT BUTTER, IF DESIRED

- ¼ cup unsalted butter, softened
- 2 tablespoons apricot preserves

HONEY HERB BUTTER, IF DESIRED

- ¼ cup unsalted butter, softened
- 2 tablespoons chopped fresh parsley
- 1 teaspoon honey

MOLASSES BUTTER, IF DESIRED

- ¼ cup unsalted butter, softened
- 2 teaspoons mild molasses

1 Heat oven to 400°F. Generously grease 32 mini muffin cups with shortening.

2 In 4-quart saucepan, heat the water and ¼ cup butter to rolling boil. Reduce heat to low; add Bisquick mix all at once. Stir vigorously with whisk about 1½ minutes or until mixture forms a ball. Remove from heat. Beat in eggs, 1 at a time; continue beating until smooth.

3 Drop dough by level measuring tablespoonfuls into muffin cups.

4 Bake 23 to 27 minutes or until deep golden brown.

5 Meanwhile, stir together ingredients of desired flavored butter(s) to serve with popovers.

1 Mini Popover (without butter): Calories 40; Total Fat 2.5g (Saturated Fat 1.5g, Trans Fat 0g); Cholesterol 25mg; Sodium 65mg; Total Carbohydrate 3g (Dietary Fiber 0g); Protein 1g **Exchanges:** ½ Fat **Carbohydrate Choices:** 0

tidbit

The batter can be made and spooned into greased mini muffin pans, covered and refrigerated up to 2 days ahead. Uncover and bake in a preheated oven for fresh popovers in minutes!

mini banana breads

PREP TIME: **20 Minutes** | START TO FINISH: **3 Hours** | **10 loaves (8 slices each)**

1¼ cups sugar

½ cup butter, softened

2 eggs

1½ cups mashed ripe bananas (3 to 4 medium)

½ cup buttermilk

1 teaspoon vanilla

2½ cups all-purpose flour

1 teaspoon baking soda

1 teaspoon salt

1 cup chopped nuts, if desired

1 Heat oven to 350°F. Grease bottoms only of 10 (4½x2½x 1½-inch) mini loaf pans with shortening or cooking spray.

2 In large bowl, mix sugar and butter with spoon. Stir in eggs until well blended. Add bananas, buttermilk and vanilla; beat until smooth. Stir in flour, baking soda and salt just until moistened. Stir in nuts. Divide batter evenly among pans, filling each with about ½ cup batter.

3 Bake 30 to 35 minutes or until toothpick inserted in centers comes out clean. Cool 5 minutes. Loosen sides of loaves from pans; transfer from pans to cooling racks. Cool completely, about 2 hours. Wrap tightly and store at room temperature up to 4 days, or refrigerate up to 7 days.

1 Slice: Calories 45; Total Fat 1.5g (Saturated Fat 1g, Trans Fat 0g); Cholesterol 10mg; Sodium 55mg; Total Carbohydrate 7g (Dietary Fiber 0g); Protein 0g **Exchanges:** ½ Other Carbohydrate, ½ Fat **Carbohydrate Choices:** ½

tidbit

Breads make tasty gifts. Package with a colorful kitchen towel or pot holder and a copy of this cookbook!

bourbon and orange mini loaves

PREP TIME: **30 Minutes** | START TO FINISH: **2 Hours 10 Minutes** | 4 loaves (4 slices each)

MINI LOAVES

- ½ cup milk
- ¼ cup bourbon
- ¼ cup butter, melted
- 1 egg
- 2 teaspoons grated orange peel
- 1½ cups all-purpose flour
- ½ cup granulated sugar
- 2 teaspoons baking powder
- ¾ teaspoon salt
- ½ cup plus 2 tablespoons chopped pecans, toasted*

GLAZE

- 2 tablespoons butter
- ¼ cup packed brown sugar
- 1 tablespoon plus 1 to 2 teaspoons milk
- ½ cup powdered sugar
- 2 teaspoons bourbon

1 Heat oven to 350°F. Grease bottoms only of 4 (4½x2½x 1½-inch) mini loaf pans with shortening or cooking spray.

2 In large bowl, stir ½ cup milk, ¼ cup bourbon, the melted butter, egg and orange peel until blended. Stir in flour, granulated sugar, baking powder and salt just until moistened. Stir in ½ cup of the pecans. Divide batter evenly among pans, about ½ cup each. Place pans on cookie sheet at least 2 inches apart.

3 Bake 30 to 35 minutes or until toothpick inserted in center comes out clean and tops begin to turn golden brown. Cool 10 minutes in pans on cooling rack.

4 Loosen sides of loaves from pans; remove from pans and place top side up on cooling rack. Cool completely, about 40 minutes.

5 Meanwhile, melt 2 tablespoons butter in 1-quart saucepan over medium heat. Stir in brown sugar. Heat to boiling, stirring constantly; reduce heat to low. Boil and stir 2 minutes. Remove from heat; stir in 1 tablespoon milk. Increase heat to medium; cook, stirring constantly, until mixture returns to a boil. Remove from heat. Place saucepan in bowl of ice water; cool to lukewarm, stirring constantly, about 2 minutes. Remove pan from ice water. Stir in powdered sugar and 2 teaspoons bourbon. Beat until smooth, adding additional milk as needed for drizzling consistency. Drizzle glaze over loaves; sprinkle with remaining 2 tablespoons pecans. Let stand 30 minutes for glaze to set. Wrap tightly and store at room temperature up to 4 days, or refrigerate up to 7 days.

* To toast pecans, sprinkle in ungreased skillet. Cook over medium-low heat 5 to 7 minutes, stirring frequently until browning begins, then stirring constantly until golden brown.

1 Slice: Calories 180; Total Fat 8g (Saturated Fat 3g, Trans Fat 0g); Cholesterol 25mg; Sodium 230mg; Total Carbohydrate 24g (Dietary Fiber 0g); Protein 2g **Exchanges:** ½ Starch, 1 Other Carbohydrate, 1½ Fat **Carbohydrate Choices:** 1½

coconut and lime mini muffins

PREP TIME: **20 Minutes** | START TO FINISH: **1 Hour** | **16 mini muffins**

MUFFINS

- ¼ cup granulated sugar
- 3 tablespoons vegetable oil
- 1 egg
- ½ cup canned coconut milk (not cream of coconut)
- 2 teaspoons grated lime peel
- ¾ cup all-purpose flour
- ¾ teaspoon baking powder
- ¼ teaspoon salt
- ¼ cup flaked coconut

GLAZE

- ½ cup powdered sugar
- 2½ teaspoons lime juice

GARNISH

- 2 tablespoons flaked coconut
- 1 teaspoon grated lime peel

1 Heat oven to 375°F. Place paper baking cup in each of 16 mini muffin cups, or grease bottoms only with shortening or cooking spray.

2 In medium bowl, stir granulated sugar, oil and egg until blended. Stir in coconut milk and 2 teaspoons lime peel until blended. Stir in flour, baking powder, salt and ¼ cup coconut just until dry ingredients are moistened. Divide batter evenly among muffin cups, filling each about three-fourths full.

3 Bake 14 to 18 minutes or until tops just begin to turn golden brown. Cool 2 to 3 minutes in pan on cooling rack; transfer from pan to cooling rack. Cool completely, about 20 minutes.

4 In small bowl, stir powdered sugar and lime juice until smooth. If necessary, stir in water, a few drops at a time, until glazing consistency; set aside.

5 In small bowl, toss 2 tablespoons coconut with 1 teaspoon lime peel. Dip top of each muffin in glaze, and let excess drip off; immediately sprinkle with coconut mixture.

1 Mini Muffin: Calories 100; Total Fat 5g (Saturated Fat 2.5g, Trans Fat 0g); Cholesterol 15mg; Sodium 70mg; Total Carbohydrate 13g (Dietary Fiber 0g); Protein 1g **Exchanges:** ½ Starch, ½ Other Carbohydrate, 1 Fat **Carbohydrate Choices:** 1

tidbits

If you have one 12-cup mini muffin pan, simply place the bowl of remaining batter in the refrigerator while the first batch of muffins bakes. Cool the pan completely before baking the remaining muffins. The cold batter might need an extra minute of bake time.

These adorable mini muffins are the perfect treat for a wedding or baby shower.

double-chocolate mini muffins

PREP TIME: 10 Minutes | **START TO FINISH: 40 Minutes** | **24 mini muffins**

1 cup all-purpose flour

⅔ cup sugar

⅓ cup unsweetened baking cocoa

½ teaspoon baking powder

½ teaspoon baking soda

¼ teaspoon salt

½ cup buttermilk

¼ cup vegetable oil

1 teaspoon vanilla

1 egg

1 cup miniature semisweet chocolate chips

1 Heat oven to 400°F. Place mini paper baking cup in each of 24 mini muffin cups.

2 In medium bowl, mix flour, sugar, cocoa, baking powder, baking soda and salt with whisk. In small bowl, mix buttermilk, oil, vanilla and egg with whisk. Add buttermilk mixture and chocolate chips to flour mixture, stirring gently until blended. Divide batter evenly among muffin cups, filling each full.

3 Bake 12 to 14 minutes or until top springs back when touched lightly in center. Cool 5 minutes; transfer from pans to cooling rack. Cool completely, about 10 minutes.

1 Mini Muffin: Calories 100; Total Fat 5g (Saturated Fat 2g); Sodium 70mg; Total Carbohydrate 15g (Dietary Fiber 1g); Protein 2g **Exchanges:** ½ Starch, ½ Other Carbohydrate, 1 Fat **Carbohydrate Choices:** 1

tidbit

Top these little muffins with chocolate frosting, and they become cupcakes!

sesame-cheddar mini muffins

PREP TIME: 15 Minutes | **START TO FINISH: 30 Minutes** | **18 mini muffins**

1 tablespoon butter

1 small sweet onion, finely chopped (⅓ cup)

1½ cups Original Bisquick mix

1 cup shredded sharp Cheddar cheese (4 oz)

1 egg

½ cup milk

1 teaspoon sesame seed, toasted*

2 tablespoons butter, melted

1 Heat oven to 400°F. Spray 18 mini muffin cups with cooking spray. In 7-inch skillet, melt 1 tablespoon butter over medium-high heat. Cook onion in butter about 2 minutes, stirring frequently, until tender. Remove from heat; set aside.

2 In large bowl, stir Bisquick mix and ½ cup of the cheese. In small bowl, stir egg, milk and onion with fork or whisk until well blended. Make well in center of Bisquick mixture; stir in egg mixture just until dry ingredients are moistened.

3 Divide batter evenly among muffin cups, filling each two-thirds full. Sprinkle evenly with remaining ½ cup cheese and the sesame seed; drizzle with 2 tablespoons melted butter.

4 Bake 12 to 14 minutes or until golden. Serve warm.

*To toast sesame seed, sprinkle in ungreased heavy skillet. Cook over medium-low heat 5 to 7 minutes, stirring frequently, until brown.

1 Mini Muffin: Calories 90; Total Fat 6g (Saturated Fat 3g, Trans Fat 0.5g); Cholesterol 25mg; Sodium 180mg; Total Carbohydrate 7g (Dietary Fiber 0g); Protein 3g **Exchanges:** ½ Starch, 1 Fat **Carbohydrate Choices:** ½

indian-spiced mini doughnut muffins

PREP TIME: 15 Minutes | **START TO FINISH:** 45 Minutes | **24 mini muffins**

⅓ cup butter

1½ cups sugar

1 egg

1½ cups all-purpose flour

1½ teaspoons baking powder

½ teaspoon salt

¼ teaspoon ground nutmeg

¼ teaspoon ground ginger

½ cup milk

1 teaspoon ground cinnamon

1 teaspoon garam masala

¼ teaspoon ground cardamom

½ cup butter, melted

1 Heat oven to 350°F. Grease 24 mini muffin cups.

2 In large bowl, beat ⅓ cup butter, ½ cup of the sugar and the egg with electric mixer on medium speed until blended. In medium bowl, mix flour, baking powder, salt, nutmeg and ginger. Add alternately with milk to butter mixture until blended. Divide batter evenly among muffin cups.

3 Bake 15 to 18 minutes or until light golden brown. Cool 5 minutes. Remove from pan.

4 In large food-storage plastic bag, mix the remaining 1 cup sugar, the cinnamon, garam masala and cardamom. Roll hot muffins in melted butter, then toss in sugar mixture to coat. Serve warm.

1 Mini Muffin: Calories 140; Total Fat 7g (Saturated Fat 4g, Trans Fat 0g); Cholesterol 25mg; Sodium 130mg; Total Carbohydrate 19g (Dietary Fiber 0g); Protein 1g **Exchanges:** 1½ Other Carbohydrate, 1 Fat **Carbohydrate Choices:** 1

tidbit

Garam masala is a wonderful Indian spice that often contains turmeric, cloves, cinnamon, pepper, cumin and cardamom. Look for jars of this spicy mixture where you buy spices.

mini beer-pimiento-cheese muffins

PREP TIME: 10 Minutes | **START TO FINISH: 35 Minutes** | **48 mini muffins**

1 bottle (12 oz) beer, room temperature

1 jar (4-oz) diced pimientos, drained

1 egg

1 teaspoon finely grated onion

4 cups Original Bisquick mix

2 cups shredded sharp Cheddar cheese (8 oz)

1 Heat oven to 400°F. Lightly spray 48 mini muffin cups with cooking spray.

2 In large bowl, mix beer, pimientos, egg and onion. Stir in Bisquick mix just until blended (batter may be lumpy). Stir in cheese. Spoon batter into muffin cups.

3 Bake 13 to 15 minutes or until lightly browned. Transfer from pan to cooling rack. Cool 10 minutes. Serve warm.

1 Mini Muffin: Calories 60; Total Fat 3g (Saturated Fat 1.5g, Trans Fat 0g); Cholesterol 10mg; Sodium 160mg; Total Carbohydrate 7g (Dietary Fiber 0g); Protein 2g **Exchanges:** ½ Starch, ½ Fat **Carbohydrate Choices:** ½

tidbit

These little muffins are a great snack or appetizer. Serve them warm in a napkin-lined basket for any occasion.

nutty whole-grain silver dollar pancakes

PREP TIME: 25 Minutes | **START TO FINISH:** 25 Minutes | 6 servings

¾   cup Wheaties cereal, slightly crushed (½ cup)

¼   cup raisins

¼   cup dry-roasted sunflower seeds

2   cups Original Bisquick mix

1½   cups Wheaties cereal, crushed (¾ cup)

1¼   cups milk

2   eggs

⅓   cup vanilla fat-free yogurt (or any other flavor)

¼   cup honey

1 In small bowl, toss ½ cup slightly crushed cereal, the raisins and sunflower seeds; set aside.

2 Heat griddle or skillet over medium heat or to 375°F. Grease griddle with vegetable oil if necessary (or spray with cooking spray before heating). In medium bowl, stir Bisquick mix, ¾ cup crushed cereal, the milk and eggs with fork until blended.

3 For each pancake, pour 1 measuring tablespoon batter onto hot griddle. Cook until edges are dry. Turn; cook other sides until golden.

4 For each serving, arrange 6 pancakes on plate. Top with 1 tablespoon yogurt and 2½ tablespoons cereal mixture. Drizzle 2 tablespoons honey over all.

1 Serving: Calories 450; Total Fat 12g (Saturated Fat 3g, Trans Fat 1g); Cholesterol 75mg; Sodium 750mg; Total Carbohydrate 79g (Dietary Fiber 2g); Protein 10g **Exchanges:** 3 Starch, 2 Other Carbohydrate, 2 Fat **Carbohydrate Choices:** 5

tidbits

Make peanut butter and jelly pancake-wiches with these little gems. Leave off the toppings, and spread with peanut butter and jelly instead.

Instead of topping with the cereal mixture, try these mini pancakes with yogurt, honey, sliced strawberries and bananas.

mini pancake-avocado stacks

PREP TIME: **1 Hour 20 Minutes** | START TO FINISH: **1 Hour 20 Minutes** | **18 servings**

1 cup Original Bisquick mix

½ cup milk

2 tablespoons real maple syrup or maple-flavored syrup

1 egg

½ cup chopped cooked bacon (about 5 slices)

¼ cup shredded Cheddar cheese (1 oz)

2 tablespoons chopped green onions

2 ripe medium avocados

1 teaspoon lemon juice

⅛ teaspoon ground red pepper (cayenne)

⅛ teaspoon salt

9 red or yellow cherry tomatoes, cut in half

1 Heat nonstick griddle to 350°F or heat 12-inch nonstick skillet over medium-low heat. (Surface is ready when a few drops of water sprinkled on it dance and disappear.)

2 In medium bowl, mix Bisquick mix, milk, syrup and egg with whisk or fork until blended. Set aside 2 tablespoons cooked bacon; stir remaining bacon, the cheese and green onions into batter.

3 For each pancake, pour batter by the teaspoonful onto hot griddle to make 54 dollar-size pancakes. Cook until edges are dry; turn and cook until golden brown.

4 Remove pits from avocados. Scoop avocado flesh into medium bowl. Add lemon juice, red pepper and salt; mash with fork until blended (mixture will be lumpy).

5 Spoon 1 teaspoon avocado mixture onto center of each of 3 pancakes. Stack pancakes, pressing down lightly on top two pancakes to spread mixture. Repeat with remaining pancakes and avocado.

6 To garnish, top each stack with reserved bacon and cherry tomato half. Secure stack with frilly toothpick. Serve immediately, or refrigerate up to 3 hours. If refrigerated, let stand at room temperature 15 minutes before serving.

1 Serving: Calories 90; Total Fat 5g (Saturated Fat 1.5g, Trans Fat 0g); Cholesterol 15mg; Sodium 170mg; Total Carbohydrate 8g (Dietary Fiber 1g); Protein 2g **Exchanges:** ½ Starch, 1 Fat **Carbohydrate Choices:** ½

tidbit

You'll want to use ripe avocados for this fun recipe. Choose those that are still firm but barely yield to gentle pressure. If they're still too hard, let them stand at room temperature for a day or two.

farmer's crostini

PREP TIME: **40 Minutes** | START TO FINISH: **40 Minutes** | **20 servings (2 crostini each)**

1 baguette (14 oz), cut into 40 (¼-inch) slices

Cooking spray

2 (3-oz) packages cream cheese, softened

¼ cup crumbled blue cheese (from 5-oz container)

¼ cup mayonnaise or salad dressing

¼ teaspoon garlic powder

¼ teaspoon salt

⅛ teaspoon pepper

½ medium cucumber, finely chopped

1 small ripe tomato, finely chopped

½ medium red or yellow bell pepper, cut into matchsticks

Fresh Italian (flat-leaf) parsley leaves, if desired

1 Heat oven to 325°F. Place bread slices on ungreased cookie sheet; spray bread lightly with cooking spray. Bake 6 to 9 minutes or until crisp. Transfer to cooling rack; cool completely.

2 In medium bowl, beat cream cheese, blue cheese, mayonnaise, garlic powder, salt and pepper with electric mixer on medium speed until well blended.

3 In small bowl, stir together cucumber, tomato and bell pepper.

4 Spread about 1 teaspoon cheese mixture on top of each slice of baguette. Top with cucumber and tomato mixture. Garnish with parsley.

1 Serving: Calories 120; Total Fat 6g (Saturated Fat 2.5g, Trans Fat 0g); Cholesterol 10mg; Sodium 230mg; Total Carbohydrate 12g (Dietary Fiber 0g); Protein 3g **Exchanges:** 1 Starch, 1 Fat **Carbohydrate Choices:** 1

tidbits

Substitute vegetables as desired. Other fresh vegetable options might include tiny broccoli florets, sliced fresh mushrooms, shredded carrot or sliced green onions.

Garnish with fresh dill sprigs or fresh thyme sprigs.

Grilled vegetables, including zucchini or summer squash, red onion strips, or bell peppers, are great on these crostini. Allow the grilled vegetables to cool slightly before placing on the cheese mixture.

fruit salsa crostini

PREP TIME: 15 Minutes | **START TO FINISH:** 15 Minutes | **32 crostini**

1 container (8 oz) pineapple
   cream cheese spread

32 thin slices French baguette

⅔ cup purchased fruit salsa

1 Spread cream cheese on baguette slices.

2 Spoon 1 teaspoon fruit salsa over cream cheese, using slotted spoon.

1 Crostini: Calories 110; Total Fat 3g (Saturated Fat 1.5g, Trans Fat 0g); Cholesterol 5mg; Sodium 230mg; Total Carbohydrate 17g (Dietary Fiber 0g); Protein 3g **Exchanges:** 1 Starch, ½ Fat **Carbohydrate Choices:** 1

tidbits

If you can't find pineapple cream cheese spread, use the plain variety instead.

Fruit salsa is also delicious served with lime-flavored tortilla chips or spooned over grilled salmon or chicken.

blt crostini

PREP TIME: **15 Minutes** | START TO FINISH: **30 Minutes** | **12 crostini**

½ cup shredded Swiss cheese (2 oz)

¼ cup mayonnaise or salad dressing

2 medium green onions, thinly sliced (2 tablespoons)

12 (¼-inch-thick) slices French baguette

6 slices refrigerated fully cooked bacon (from 2.1 oz package), cut in half

¼ cup finely shredded iceberg lettuce

4 cherry tomatoes, each cut into 3 slices

1 Heat oven to 375°F. In small bowl, mix cheese, mayonnaise and onions. Spread about 1 teaspoon cheese mixture on each bread slice; place on ungreased cookie sheet. Top each with half slice bacon.

2 Bake 10 to 12 minutes or until edges of bread are golden brown and cheese is melted.

3 Garnish each crostini with lettuce and tomato slice.

1 Crostini: Calories 80; Total Fat 6g (Saturated Fat 2g, Trans Fat 0g); Cholesterol 10mg; Sodium 120mg; Total Carbohydrate 5g (Dietary Fiber 0g); Protein 3g **Exchanges:** ½ Starch, 1 Fat **Carbohydrate Choices:** ½

tidbits

For extra flavor, try rubbing these crostini with cut garlic cloves before spreading them with the cheese mixture.

Look for bags of shredded lettuce in the produce section of your supermarket. Or, you can use small pieces of torn leaf lettuce or even romaine instead of the shredded lettuce.

apple-bacon-cheddar crostini

PREP TIME: 35 Minutes | START TO FINISH: **50 Minutes** | **24 crostini**

6 slices bacon

4 cups finely chopped peeled apples (3 medium)

1 teaspoon grated gingerroot

¼ cup packed brown sugar

1 tablespoon fresh thyme leaves

½ teaspoon salt

2 tablespoons apple juice

24 (½-inch-thick) slices French baguette

2 tablespoons olive oil

1½ cups shredded sharp Cheddar cheese (6 oz)

Fresh thyme sprigs, if desired

1 In 12-inch nonstick skillet, cook bacon until crisp; drain on paper towels. Crumble bacon; set aside. Reserve drippings in skillet.

2 Cook apples and gingerroot in bacon drippings over medium-high heat, stirring occasionally, until lightly browned and tender. Stir in brown sugar, thyme and salt. Cook 1 minute; stir in apple juice. Cook 1 minute; remove from heat. Cool completely.

3 Heat oven to 450°F. Place baguette slices in single layer on ungreased cookie sheet. Brush with 1 tablespoon of the oil. Bake 3 to 5 minutes or until toasted. Turn slices over; brush with remaining 1 tablespoon oil. Bake 3 to 5 minutes longer or until toasted.

4 In skillet, add cheese and bacon to apples; toss. Place about 1 tablespoon apple mixture on each baguette slice. Bake 5 minutes or until cheese is melted. Garnish with thyme sprigs. Serve immediately.

1 Crostini: Calories 100; Total Fat 4.5g (Saturated Fat 2g, Trans Fat 0g); Cholesterol 10mg; Sodium 190mg; Total Carbohydrate 10g (Dietary Fiber 0g); Protein 3g **Exchanges:** ½ Starch, 1 Fat **Carbohydrate Choices:** ½

mini meals

Dazzle your guests with these teeny main dishes. Pick and choose your favorites to create a fun and delicious meal!

mini breakfast quiches with potato crust

PREP TIME: **20 Minutes** | START TO FINISH: **1 Hour** | **6 servings (2 mini quiches each)**

1 box (4.5-oz) seasoned traditional recipe skillet potatoes

   Water and vegetable oil called for on potato box

½ cup crumbled cooked bacon

½ cup shredded Swiss cheese (2 oz)

3 eggs

1 cup whipping cream

1 Heat oven to 350°F. Spray 12 regular-size muffin cups with cooking spray.

2 Make potatoes as directed on box, using water and oil. Divide potato mixture evenly among muffin cups, pressing in bottom and up side of each cup to form crust. Sprinkle bacon and cheese evenly in cups.

3 In medium bowl, beat eggs and cream. Pour filling evenly into cups, about ¼ cup each.

4 Bake 25 to 30 minutes or until knife inserted in center comes out clean. Let stand 10 minutes before serving.

1 Serving: Calories 360; Total Fat 28g (Saturated Fat 12g, Trans Fat 0.5g); Cholesterol 165mg; Sodium 590mg; Total Carbohydrate 19g (Dietary Fiber 1g); Protein 10g **Exchanges:** 1½ Starch, ½ Medium-Fat Meat, 4½ Fat **Carbohydrate Choices:** 1

tidbits

If you want vegetables instead of bacon, try substituting ¼ cup cooked and drained spinach for a delicious variation.

Try another variation by substituting your favorite fillings, such as ham and Cheddar cheese.

creamy tomato-basil soup with mini grilled cheese sandwiches

PREP TIME: **40 Minutes** | START TO FINISH: **40 Minutes** | **9 servings**

TOMATO SOUP

- ¼ cup olive oil
- 1 medium onion, chopped (½ cup)
- 1 clove garlic, finely chopped
- 2 cans (14.5-oz each) diced tomatoes, undrained
- 1 container (5.3 oz) plain Greek yogurt
- ¼ cup grated Parmesan cheese (1 oz)
- 2 tablespoons chopped fresh basil leaves
- ½ teaspoon salt
- ¼ teaspoon pepper

SANDWICHES

- 3 tablespoons butter, softened
- 6 (½-inch-thick) slices whole-grain bread
- 3 slices (1 oz each) Cheddar cheese, cut in half
- 1 tablespoon chopped fresh basil leaves
- 9 (4-inch) wooden skewers

1 In 4-quart saucepan, heat oil, onion and garlic over medium-low heat 5 to 10 minutes, stirring frequently, until onion is soft and translucent.

2 Add tomatoes; heat to boiling. Reduce heat; simmer 30 minutes, stirring occasionally. Remove from heat; add yogurt, Parmesan cheese, 2 tablespoons basil leaves, the salt and pepper. In blender, place soup mixture. Cover; puree until smooth.

3 Spread butter on 1 side of each bread slice. Arrange 3 slices bread, buttered side down, on work surface; place 2 slices cheese and 1 teaspoon of the basil leaves on each bread slice. Top with remaining 3 bread slices, buttered sides up. In 10-inch nonstick skillet, cook 3 sandwiches at a time over medium heat, turning once, until golden brown and cheese just melts. Cut each sandwich into 6 squares. Place 2 sandwich squares onto each skewer.

4 To serve, spoon ½ cup soup into each of 9 small cups; place sandwich skewer on top of cup.

1 Serving: Calories 220; Total Fat 14g (Saturated Fat 6g, Trans Fat 0g); Cholesterol 25mg; Sodium 500mg; Total Carbohydrate 14g (Dietary Fiber 2g); Protein 8g **Exchanges:** 1 Starch, ½ Lean Meat, 2½ Fat **Carbohydrate Choices:** 1

tidbit

Prepare the soup a day ahead, cover and refrigerate. Reheat over medium-low heat, stirring occasionally, 5 to 8 minutes or until thoroughly heated.

triple-decker mini reubens

PREP TIME: 55 Minutes | START TO FINISH: **55 Minutes** | **24 mini sandwiches**

3 long slices (1½ oz each) Swiss cheese

18 slices rye bread, crusts removed

2 tablespoons Thousand Island dressing

½ cup butter, melted

2 tablespoons spicy brown mustard

6 oz shaved pastrami (from deli)

1½ cups refrigerated sauerkraut (from 25-oz jar), squeezed to drain

6 oz shaved corned beef (from deli)

24 cornichons in vinegar, if desired

24 (6-inch) bamboo skewers

1 Cut each slice of cheese in half crosswise, then cut each half diagonally to form 2 triangles.

2 Toast 6 bread slices; spread dressing evenly over 1 side of each slice. Brush melted butter over 1 side of each slice of remaining untoasted bread. Place 6 bread slices, buttered side down, on work surface; spread each with 1 teaspoon mustard. Divide pastrami evenly over mustard-coated bread slices; top each with 2 tablespoons sauerkraut, 1 cheese triangle and 1 toasted bread slice, dressing side up. Divide corned beef evenly over dressing-coated bread slices; top each with 2 tablespoons sauerkraut, 1 cheese triangle and remaining bread slices, buttered side up. Secure sandwiches with toothpicks.

3 Heat 12-inch nonstick skillet or griddle over medium heat. Cook sandwiches 6 to 10 minutes, turning once, until lightly browned and cheese is melted.

4 Using electric knife or serrated knife, carefully cut each sandwich into 4 rectangles. Secure each mini sandwich with 6-inch bamboo skewer. Garnish with cornichons.

1 Mini Sandwich: Calories 150; Total Fat 8g (Saturated Fat 4g, Trans Fat 0g); Cholesterol 25mg; Sodium 510mg; Total Carbohydrate 13g (Dietary Fiber 1g); Protein 6g **Exchanges:** 1 Starch, ½ Medium-Fat Meat, 1 Fat **Carbohydrate Choices:** 1

meatball mini burgers

PREP TIME: **45 Minutes** | START TO FINISH: **45 Minutes** | **32 mini burgers**

TINY BUNS

1   can (16.3 oz) large refrigerated buttermilk or original flaky biscuits (8 biscuits)

1   egg

1   tablespoon water

2   tablespoons sesame seed

MEATBALLS

2   teaspoons vegetable oil

½   cup chopped onion (1 medium)

¾   cup chili sauce

¼   cup water

¼   cup yellow mustard

2   teaspoons chili powder

32   frozen plain meatballs (from 28-oz package; about 3 cups), thawed

8   slices (¾ oz each) American cheese, cut into quarters

1   Heat oven to 350°F. On ungreased cookie sheet, place biscuits 1 to 2 inches apart. Cut each biscuit into quarters, but do not separate pieces. In small bowl, beat egg and 1 tablespoon water. Brush egg mixture over tops of biscuits; sprinkle with sesame seed.

2   Bake 14 to 17 minutes or until golden brown. Cool slightly; separate biscuit quarters.

3   Meanwhile, in 2-quart saucepan, heat oil over medium-high heat. Add onion; cook, stirring frequently, until onion is tender. Stir in chili sauce, ¼ cup water, the mustard and chili powder. Cook 3 to 5 minutes, stirring frequently, until slightly thickened.

4   Add meatballs to chili sauce mixture. Cover; cook over medium heat 8 to 10 minutes, stirring occasionally, until meatballs are hot.

5   Split each biscuit quarter to make tiny bun. Fill each bun with 1 cheese piece, 1 meatball and some of the sauce. Secure with toothpicks.

1 Mini Burger: Calories 150; Total Fat 8g (Saturated Fat 3g, Trans Fat 1g); Cholesterol 40mg; Sodium 470mg; Total Carbohydrate 11g (Dietary Fiber 1g); Protein 8g **Exchanges:** ½ Starch, 1 High-Fat Meat **Carbohydrate Choices:** 1

tidbits

Experiment with different cheeses, such as Cheddar, Gouda or Monterey Jack with jalapeño peppers, to create a new flavor combination.

To save time, purchase dinner rolls or dollar buns instead of making your own.

mini greek burgers

PREP TIME: **30 Minutes** | START TO FINISH: **30 Minutes** | **16 mini burgers**

SAUCE

- ¾ cup plain fat-free yogurt
- 1 teaspoon grated lemon peel
- 1 clove garlic, finely chopped
- ¼ teaspoon salt
- ¼ teaspoon dried dill weed

BURGERS

- 1 lb lean (at least 80%) ground beef
- ¼ cup plain bread crumbs
- 1 tablespoon balsamic vinegar
- 2 teaspoons finely grated lemon peel
- 2 teaspoons fresh lemon juice
- 1 teaspoon dried oregano leaves
- 1 teaspoon dried thyme leaves
- ½ teaspoon salt
- 3 cloves garlic, finely chopped

BREADS AND TOPPINGS

- 16 mini (2½-inch) pita breads (from 7-oz bag)
- ½ medium cucumber, cut into very thin slices
- ¼ small red onion, cut into bite-size strips

1 In small bowl, mix sauce ingredients. Cover; refrigerate until ready to use.

2 In large bowl, mix burger ingredients until well mixed. Shape mixture into 16 patties, about ¼ inch thick.

3 Place 8 patties in 12-inch nonstick skillet; cook over medium-low heat about 3 minutes. Turn patties; cook 2 to 4 minutes longer or until meat thermometer inserted in center of patties reads 160°F. Remove patties from skillet; cover to keep warm. Repeat with remaining patties.

4 With serrated knife, cut pita breads in half horizontally. Place patties on bottom halves of breads. Top each patty with about 2 teaspoons sauce, several slices of cucumber and strips of onion. Cover with top halves of breads. Serve immediately.

1 Mini Burger: Calories 90; Total Fat 3.5g (Saturated Fat 1.5g, Trans Fat 0g); Cholesterol 20mg; Sodium 190mg; Total Carbohydrate 8g (Dietary Fiber 0g); Protein 6g **Exchanges:** ½ Starch, ½ Medium-Fat Meat **Carbohydrate Choices:** ½

tidbit

Look for mini pitas in the deli or bakery section of your grocery store. If you can't find mini pita breads, purchase regular-size ones and cut them into quarters.

whiskey and beer bbq chicken sliders

PREP TIME: **20 Minutes** | START TO FINISH: **40 Minutes** | **12 sliders**

SAUCE

- 1 cup barbecue sauce
- 1½ cups lager beer, such as a pilsner
- 2 tablespoons whiskey
- 1 teaspoon seasoned salt
- 1 teaspoon garlic-pepper blend
- ½ teaspoon ground mustard
- 1 to 2 teaspoons Buffalo wing sauce or other hot sauce

SANDWICHES

- 1 deli rotisserie chicken, skin and bones removed, shredded (about 4 cups)
- 12 mini burger or slider buns (about 2½ inches in diameter), split
- 12 pimiento-stuffed green olives, if desired

1 In 2-quart saucepan, heat sauce ingredients to boiling over medium heat, stirring frequently. Reduce heat to medium-low and simmer 20 minutes, stirring occasionally to prevent scorching.

2 In medium microwavable bowl, place chicken; cover. Microwave on High 4 to 5 minutes or until hot. Add shredded chicken to sauce in saucepan; stir to coat.

3 Place about ⅓ cup chicken mixture on bottom of each slider bun; top with bun top. Garnish each sandwich with 1 olive.

1 Slider: Calories 230; Total Fat 6g (Saturated Fat 1.5g, Trans Fat 0g); Cholesterol 40mg; Sodium 620mg; Total Carbohydrate 25g (Dietary Fiber 0g); Protein 16g **Exchanges:** 1½ Starch, 2 Lean Meat **Carbohydrate Choices:** 1½

spiced sweet potato–turkey sliders

PREP TIME: **40 Minutes** | START TO FINISH: **55 Minutes** | **12 sliders**

PATTIES

- 1 lb lean ground turkey or lean (at least 80%) ground beef
- 1 tablespoon chopped green onion
- 1 teaspoon garam masala
- 1 teaspoon red curry paste
- ½ teaspoon ground cumin
- ½ teaspoon salt

SWEET POTATOES

- 1 small dark-orange sweet potato, peeled, cut into ¼-inch slices
- 1 tablespoon olive oil
- 1 teaspoon garam masala
- ½ teaspoon ground cumin
- ¼ teaspoon salt

TOPPINGS AND BUNS

- ¾ cup mayonnaise
- 2 teaspoons red curry paste
- 12 mini burger or slider buns (about 2½ inches in diameter), split, toasted if desired
- 6 leaves Bibb lettuce, each cut in half
- 2 plum (Roma) tomatoes, cut into 12 slices

  Fresh cilantro leaves, if desired

1 Heat oven to 450°F. Line bottom of 15x10x1-inch pan with foil; spray with cooking spray. In medium bowl, mix patty ingredients until well combined. Divide into 12 equal portions. Shape each portion into a ball; flatten each until about 2½ inches in diameter. Place patties close together in half of pan.

2 In large bowl, stir sweet potato ingredients until evenly coated. Place sweet potato slices in other half of pan, overlapping slightly if necessary.

3 Bake 12 to 14 minutes, turning patties and slices once, until patties are no longer pink in center (165°F) and potatoes are tender.

4 Meanwhile, in small bowl, stir mayonnaise and 2 teaspoons red curry paste until blended.

5 On bottom half of each bun, place 1 lettuce piece, 1 to 2 sweet potato slices, 1 patty, 1 tomato slice, cilantro and scant 1 tablespoon mayonnaise mixture. Cover with top halves of buns.

1 Slider: Calories 260; Total Fat 16g (Saturated Fat 3g, Trans Fat 0g); Cholesterol 35mg; Sodium 440mg; Total Carbohydrate 17g (Dietary Fiber 1g); Protein 10g **Exchanges:** 1 Starch, 1 Lean Meat, 2½ Fat **Carbohydrate Choices:** 1

tidbit

If you moisten your hands with water before forming the patties, the meat will be easier to shape and won't stick to your hands.

black bean sliders

PREP TIME: **45 Minutes** | START TO FINISH: **2 Hours 45 Minutes** | **20 sliders**

BUNS

5 frozen stone-ground 100% whole wheat Texas rolls (from 3-lb bag)

2 tablespoons butter, melted

SALSA

1 can (7 oz) whole kernel corn with red and green peppers, drained

2/3 cup chunky-style medium salsa

BEAN PATTIES

5 teaspoons olive oil

1/4 cup finely chopped red or yellow onion

1 can (15 oz) black beans, drained, rinsed

1 egg, beaten

1/2 cup plain bread crumbs

2 cloves garlic, finely chopped

1 teaspoon ground cumin

1/2 teaspoon salt

1/4 teaspoon freshly ground pepper

Bibb or leaf lettuce, torn into 20 small pieces

5 slices (3/4 oz each) Cheddar cheese, cut into quarters

1 Thaw rolls at room temperature until soft but still cold, about 10 minutes. Spray cookie sheet with cooking spray. Cut each roll into quarters; shape dough pieces into balls. Place on cookie sheet. Brush tops of dough balls with butter. Cover with plastic wrap sprayed with cooking spray. Let rise in warm place 2 hours to 2 hours 30 minutes until doubled in size.

2 Heat oven to 350°F. Remove plastic wrap. Bake buns 12 to 15 minutes or until golden brown. Remove from pan to cooling rack.

3 Meanwhile, in medium bowl, mix salsa ingredients. Cover; refrigerate until serving time.

4 In 10-inch nonstick skillet, heat 1 teaspoon of the oil over medium heat. Add onion; cook 3 to 4 minutes, stirring frequently, until softened. Remove from heat; cool slightly.

5 In medium bowl, mash beans with potato masher or fork, leaving a few beans whole. Stir in egg, bread crumbs, garlic, cumin, salt and pepper. Add cooled onion; mix until thoroughly combined. Shape mixture into 20 (1-inch) balls, using slightly less than 1 tablespoon per ball.

6 In same skillet, heat 2 teaspoons oil over medium heat. Place half of the bean balls in skillet; with back of spatula, flatten balls into patties, about 1½ inches in diameter. Cook 4 to 6 minutes, turning once, until browned. Remove from skillet; cover to keep warm. Repeat with remaining 2 teaspoons oil and bean balls.

7 Split buns in half. On bottom half of each bun, place lettuce piece, bean patty, cheese quarter and 1 heaping tablespoon salsa. Cover with top halves of buns.

1 Slider: Calories 130; Total Fat 5g (Saturated Fat 2g, Trans Fat 0g); Cholesterol 20mg; Sodium 270mg; Total Carbohydrate 17g (Dietary Fiber 3g); Protein 5g **Exchanges:** 1 Starch, ½ Vegetable, 1 Fat **Carbohydrate Choices:** 1

tidbit

Try white beans — cannellini beans or chickpeas (garbanzo beans) — as an alternative to the black beans.

impossibly easy mini blue cheeseburger pies

PREP TIME: **15 Minutes** | START TO FINISH: **1 Hour 5 Minutes** | **6 servings (2 mini pies each)**

BURGER MIXTURE

- 1 lb lean (at least 80%) ground beef
- 1 large onion, chopped (1 cup)
- ½ cup crumbled blue cheese (2 oz)
- 2 teaspoons Worcestershire sauce

BAKING MIXTURE

- ½ cup Original Bisquick mix
- ½ cup milk
- 2 eggs

TOPPING

- 6 tablespoons French-fried onions (from 2.8-oz can)

1 Heat oven to 375°F. Spray 12 regular-size muffin cups with cooking spray.

2 In 10-inch skillet, cook beef and onion over medium-high heat 5 to 7 minutes, stirring occasionally, until beef is thoroughly cooked; drain. Cool 5 minutes; stir in cheese and Worcestershire sauce.

3 In medium bowl, stir baking mixture ingredients with whisk or fork until blended. Spoon slightly less than 1 tablespoon baking mixture into each muffin cup. Top each with about ¼ cup burger mixture and 1 tablespoon baking mixture.

4 Bake 10 minutes. Sprinkle evenly with French-fried onions. Bake 15 to 20 minutes longer or until toothpick inserted in center comes out clean and tops are golden brown. Cool 5 minutes. With thin knife, loosen sides of pies from pan; remove from pan and place top sides up on cooling rack. Cool 10 minutes longer before serving.

1 Serving: Calories 280; Total Fat 17g (Saturated Fat 7g, Trans Fat 1.5g); Cholesterol 120mg; Sodium 390mg; Total Carbohydrate 12g (Dietary Fiber 0g); Protein 19g **Exchanges:** ½ Starch, ½ Vegetable, 2½ Lean Meat, 2 Fat **Carbohydrate Choices:** 1

muffin tin taco pies

PREP TIME: **30 Minutes** | START TO FINISH: **1 Hour 15 Minutes** | **6 servings (2 pies each)**

CRUST

1	box refrigerated pie crusts, softened as directed on box
1	egg white
½	teaspoon ground cumin

FILLING

1	lb lean (at least 80%) ground beef
1	medium onion, finely chopped (¾ cup)
1	package (1 oz) 40% less sodium taco seasoning mix
½	cup chunky-style salsa
⅓	cup water
1	cup shredded Mexican cheese blend (4 oz)
¼	cup chopped fresh cilantro

TOPPINGS, IF DESIRED

Sour cream

Salsa

Sliced jalapeño chiles

Sliced ripe olives

Shredded lettuce

Chopped avocado

Chopped tomato

1 Heat oven to 400°F. On floured surface and using floured rolling pin, roll each piecrust to 12-inch round. Cut into 12 (4-inch) rounds. Firmly press rounds in bottoms and up sides of 12 ungreased regular-size muffin cups. In small bowl, beat egg white and cumin with whisk until frothy. Generously brush mixture over insides of each pastry-lined cup.

2 In 10-inch nonstick skillet, cook beef over medium-high heat 5 minutes. Add onion. Reduce heat to medium. Cook 3 minutes longer, stirring occasionally, until beef is thoroughly cooked; drain. Stir in taco seasoning mix, salsa and water. Cook over medium heat 5 minutes, stirring occasionally, until slightly thickened. Spoon hot beef mixture evenly into muffin cups.

3 Bake 30 to 35 minutes or until crust edges are golden brown. Sprinkle tops of pies with cheese. Bake 2 to 3 minutes longer or until cheese is melted. Let stand 5 minutes before serving. Sprinkle with cilantro. Serve with toppings.

1 Serving: Calories 590; Total Fat 37g (Saturated Fat 13g, Trans Fat 1g); Cholesterol 65mg; Sodium 1,020mg; Total Carbohydrate 40g (Dietary Fiber 1g); Protein 23g **Exchanges:** 2½ Starch, 1½ Medium-Fat Meat, ½ High-Fat Meat, 5 Fat **Carbohydrate Choices:** 2½

tidbit

Brushing the pastry with an egg white before adding the filling helps seal the crust, keeping the dough crisp and flaky. This technique is particularly useful with a moist filling like this one.

impossibly easy mini chicken pot pies

PREP TIME: **20 Minutes** | START TO FINISH: **1 Hour** | **6 servings (2 mini pies each)**

CHICKEN MIXTURE

- 1 tablespoon vegetable oil
- 1 lb boneless skinless chicken breasts, cut into bite-size pieces
- 1 medium onion, chopped (½ cup)
- ½ cup chicken broth
- 1 cup frozen peas and carrots
- ½ teaspoon salt
- ¼ teaspoon pepper
- ¼ teaspoon ground thyme
- 1 cup shredded Cheddar cheese (4 oz)

BAKING MIXTURE

- ½ cup Original Bisquick mix
- ½ cup milk
- 2 eggs

1 Heat oven to 375°F. Spray 12 regular-size muffin cups with cooking spray.

2 In 10-inch nonstick skillet, heat oil over medium-high heat. Cook chicken in oil 5 to 7 minutes, stirring occasionally, until chicken is no longer pink in center. Add onion and chicken broth; heat to simmering. Add frozen vegetables and seasonings. Heat until hot, stirring occasionally until almost all liquid is absorbed. Cool 5 minutes; stir in cheese.

3 In medium bowl, stir baking mixture ingredients with whisk or fork until blended. Spoon slightly less than 1 tablespoon baking mixture into each muffin cup. Top with about ¼ cup chicken mixture. Spoon 1 tablespoon baking mixture onto chicken mixture in each muffin cup.

4 Bake 25 to 30 minutes or until toothpick inserted in center comes out clean. Cool 5 minutes. With thin knife, loosen sides of pies from pan; remove from pan and place top side up on cooling rack. Cool 10 minutes longer.

1 Serving: Calories 290; Total Fat 15g (Saturated Fat 6g, Trans Fat 0.5g); Cholesterol 130mg; Sodium 600mg; Total Carbohydrate 12g (Dietary Fiber 1g); Protein 26g **Exchanges:** ½ Starch, ½ Vegetable, 3 Very Lean Meat, ½ High-Fat Meat, 2 Fat **Carbohydrate Choices:** 1

sriracha veggie-cheese balls and sauce

PREP TIME: **25 Minutes** | START TO FINISH: **50 Minutes** | **25 servings**

VEGGIE-CHEESE BALLS

- 2 cups frozen chopped broccoli, thawed, squeezed to drain
- 2 cups shredded Colby–Monterey Jack cheese blend (8 oz)
- 1 cup Original Bisquick mix
- 1 egg
- 1 tablespoon finely chopped red bell pepper
- 1 teaspoon garlic salt
- 1 to 2 teaspoons sriracha sauce

DIPPING SAUCE

- ½ cup sour cream
- 2 teaspoons sriracha sauce
- 2 tablespoons sliced green onions (2 medium)
- 2 tablespoons finely chopped red bell pepper

1 Heat oven to 350°F. Spray or grease bottom and sides of 15x10x1-inch pan.

2 In large bowl, stir together veggie-cheese ball ingredients. Slightly moisten hands with water for easier rolling; shape mixture into 25 (1-inch) balls; place on pan.

3 Bake 20 to 25 minutes or until golden brown. Meanwhile, in small bowl, mix dipping sauce ingredients.

4 Immediately remove balls from pan. Serve warm with sauce for dipping.

1 Serving: Calories 70 (Calories from Fat 40); Total Fat 4.5g (Saturated Fat 2.5g, Trans Fat 0g); Cholesterol 20mg; Sodium 170mg; Total Carbohydrate 4g (Dietary Fiber 0g); Protein 3g **Exchanges:** ½ Starch, 1 Fat **Carbohydrate Choices:** 0

tidbit

Here are several make-ahead options for the recipe:

- Cover and refrigerate unbaked veggie-cheese balls up to 24 hours. Bake as directed.

- Cover and freeze unbaked veggie-cheese balls for up to 1 month. Bake at 350°F on ungreased cookie sheet for 25 to 30 minutes or until brown.

- Bake the veggie-cheese balls as directed; cover and freeze for up to 1 month. Bake at 350°F on ungreased cookie sheet for 10 to 12 minutes or until thoroughly heated.

- Bake the veggie-cheese balls as directed; cover and freeze for up to 1 month. Place 6 frozen balls on microwavable plate. Loosely cover with waxed paper. Microwave on High 45 to 60 seconds or until thoroughly heated.

bacon, kale and egg cups

PREP TIME: **30 Minutes** | START TO FINISH: **1 Hour** | **12 servings**

3 large kale leaves

6 slices cooked bacon, each cut in half crosswise

¼ cup finely chopped red bell pepper

1 tablespoon chopped green onion

3 tablespoons grated Parmesan cheese

12 eggs

¼ teaspoon salt

⅛ teaspoon pepper

Additional grated Parmesan cheese, if desired

1 Heat oven to 350°F. Lightly grease 12 regular-size muffin cups with shortening.

2 Cut kale into 2- to 3-inch pieces. In 2-quart saucepan, heat ½ inch water to boiling. Add kale pieces; cover and cook about 5 minutes or until bright green and just tender.

3 Line bottom and side of each muffin cup with several small leaves of steamed kale (leaves should stick up around edge of cup). Place ½ bacon slice in each cup over kale.

4 In small bowl, stir together bell pepper and green onion; reserve 1 tablespoon. Stir cheese into remaining bell pepper and onion. Place about 1 teaspoon vegetable-cheese mixture into each muffin cup. Press mixture down slightly with back of spoon. Break egg into small custard cup; slide into muffin cup over cheese mixture. Top with reserved bell pepper and onion. Season with salt and pepper; sprinkle with additional cheese.

5 Bake 25 to 30 minutes or until egg yolks are set. Serve immediately.

1 Serving: Calories 110; Total Fat 7g (Saturated Fat 2.5g, Trans Fat 0g); Cholesterol 190mg; Sodium 230mg; Total Carbohydrate 1g (Dietary Fiber 0g); Protein 8g **Exchanges:** 1 Medium-Fat Meat, ½ Fat **Carbohydrate Choices:** 0

tidbit

Cooked bacon is usually available in the deli meat area of the grocery store. If you choose to cook your own, just allow a bit of extra time to make the recipe.

impossibly easy brussels sprouts mini pies

PREP TIME: **20 Minutes** | START TO FINISH: **55 Minutes** | **6 servings (2 mini pies each)**

1 box (10 oz) frozen baby Brussels sprouts and butter sauce

½ cup chopped fresh mushrooms

¼ teaspoon dried thyme leaves

⅛ teaspoon pepper

½ cup Original Bisquick mix

½ cup milk

2 eggs

¾ cup shredded Swiss cheese (3 oz)

1 Heat oven to 375°F. Spray 12 regular-size muffin cups with cooking spray.

2 Cook Brussels sprouts for the minimum time as directed on box; pour into medium bowl. Cool 5 minutes. Cut Brussels sprouts in half. Stir in mushrooms, thyme and pepper.

3 In medium bowl, stir Bisquick mix, milk and eggs with whisk or fork until blended. Spoon slightly less than 1 tablespoon batter into each muffin cup. Divide Brussels sprouts mixture evenly among cups; sprinkle each with about 1 tablespoon cheese. Top each with 1 tablespoon batter.

4 Bake 22 to 27 minutes or until toothpick inserted in center comes out clean and tops are golden brown. Cool 5 minutes. With thin knife, loosen sides of pies from pan; transfer from pan to cooling rack. Serve warm.

1 Serving: Calories 160; Total Fat 8g (Saturated Fat 4g, Trans Fat 0g); Cholesterol 80mg; Sodium 320mg; Total Carbohydrate 13g (Dietary Fiber 1g); Protein 9g **Exchanges:** ½ Starch, ½ Other Carbohydrate, ½ Lean Meat, ½ High-Fat Meat, ½ Fat **Carbohydrate Choices:** 1

tidbits

For a little added "heat," stir ¼ to ½ teaspoon hot pepper sauce into the Brussels sprouts mixture.

The pies can be covered and refrigerated up to 24 hours before baking. You may need to bake a bit longer than the recipe directs, since you'll be starting with a cold pie. Watch carefully for doneness.

mini corn cakes

PREP TIME: 25 Minutes | **START TO FINISH: 25 Minutes** | **24 servings**

1 tablespoon butter

⅓ cup chopped green onions (about 5 medium)

⅓ cup chopped celery

⅓ cup chopped red bell pepper

1 cup soft white bread crumbs (about 1½ slices bread)

½ cup Original Bisquick mix

1 teaspoon sugar

½ teaspoon salt

⅛ teaspoon ground red pepper (cayenne)

2 eggs, slightly beaten

1 can (11 oz) whole kernel sweet corn, drained

2 tablespoons vegetable oil

½ cup chive-and-onion sour cream potato topper (from 12-oz container)

1 In 12-inch nonstick skillet, melt butter over medium heat. Cook onions, celery and bell pepper in butter 3 minutes, stirring occasionally.

2 In medium bowl, stir vegetable mixture, bread crumbs, Bisquick mix, sugar, salt, red pepper, eggs and corn until well blended.

3 In same skillet, heat 2 teaspoons of the oil over medium heat. Drop 8 tablespoonfuls of corn mixture into oil, spreading each to 1½-inch round. Cook 2 to 3 minutes, carefully turning once, until golden brown. Cook remaining corn cakes in 2 batches of 8 each, using 2 teaspoons oil for each batch. Serve with sour cream topper.

1 Serving: Calories 60; Total Fat 3.5g (Saturated Fat 1.5g, Trans Fat 0g); Cholesterol 20mg; Sodium 135mg; Total Carbohydrate 5g (Dietary Fiber 0g); Protein 1g **Exchanges:** ½ Starch, ½ Fat **Carbohydrate Choices:** ½

lasagna cupcakes

PREP TIME: 15 Minutes | **START TO FINISH:** 1 Hour | **12 servings**

1   cup ricotta cheese

½   cup grated Parmesan cheese

1   egg

1   jar (25.5 oz) organic pasta sauce (any variety)

8   oz frozen Italian sausage–style soy protein crumbles (2 cups)

36   round pot sticker (gyoza) wrappers

1   cup shredded mozzarella cheese (4 oz)

1 Heat oven to 375°F. Spray 12 regular-size muffin cups with cooking spray. In small bowl, mix ricotta cheese, Parmesan cheese and egg. In another small bowl, mix pasta sauce and soy protein crumbles.

2 Place 1 round wrapper in bottom of each muffin cup; top each with 1 heaping tablespoon pasta sauce mixture and 1 tablespoon cheese mixture. Repeat layers, ending with pasta sauce mixture. Sprinkle each with mozzarella cheese.

3 Spray large sheet of foil with cooking spray; place sprayed side down over pan. Bake 15 minutes. Uncover; bake 15 minutes longer. Let stand about 15 minutes before serving.

1 Serving: Calories 170; Total Fat 7g (Saturated Fat 3g, Trans Fat 0g); Cholesterol 30mg; Sodium 500mg; Total Carbohydrate 13g (Dietary Fiber 2g); Protein 12g **Exchanges:** 1 Starch, 1 Medium-Fat Meat **Carbohydrate Choices:** 1

tidbits

These are fantastic little casseroles to freeze and eat for a quick dinner or to take to work for lunch. Microwave 1 frozen cupcake, uncovered, on Medium (50%) 5 to 6 minutes or until hot.

If desired, layer small, whole fresh basil leaves in the center of each lasagna cupcake.

taco mac cupcakes

PREP TIME: **25 Minutes** | START TO FINISH: **35 Minutes** | **18 servings**

18 wonton skins (about 3¼-inch square)

1 package (20 oz) refrigerated macaroni and cheese

1 lb lean (at least 80%) ground beef

1 medium onion, chopped (½ cup)

½ cup chopped green bell pepper

1 package (1 oz) taco seasoning mix

¼ cup water

1 cup shredded Mexican cheese blend (4 oz)

½ cup sour cream

½ cup sliced green onions (8 medium)

½ cup sliced ripe olives

1 Heat oven to 400°F. Spray 18 regular-size muffin cups with cooking spray. Place 1 wonton skin in each muffin cup, pressing down slightly. Bake about 8 minutes or until golden brown.

2 Meanwhile, cook macaroni and cheese as directed on package; keep warm.

3 In 12-inch skillet, cook beef, onion and bell pepper over medium-high heat 5 to 7 minutes, stirring occasionally, until beef is thoroughly cooked; drain. Stir in taco seasoning mix and water. Add macaroni and cheese; mix well. Spoon ¼ cup taco mixture into each wonton cup. Sprinkle evenly with cheese.

4 Bake about 2 minutes or until cheese is melted. Cool 5 minutes. Remove from pan. Top each taco cup with sour cream, green onions and olives. Serve warm.

1 Serving: Calories 140; Total Fat 7g (Saturated Fat 3.5g, Trans Fat 0g); Cholesterol 25mg; Sodium 380mg; Total Carbohydrate 12g (Dietary Fiber 1g); Protein 8g **Exchanges:** 1 Other Carbohydrate, 1 High-Fat Meat **Carbohydrate Choices:** 1

tidbit

You can easily substitute 2 cups shredded deli rotisserie chicken for the beef if you prefer.

chicken pot pie cupcakes

PREP TIME: 15 Minutes | **START TO FINISH:** 45 Minutes | 12 servings

1 can (18.5 oz) ready-to-serve chicken pot pie–style soup

1/3 cup plain mashed potato mix (dry)

1/2 cup frozen mixed vegetables, cooked

1/4 teaspoon dried thyme leaves

1/4 teaspoon pepper

2 cans (8 oz each) refrigerated flaky dough sheet

1 tablespoon butter, melted

1 Heat oven to 375°F. Spray 12 regular-size muffin cups with cooking spray.

2 In medium bowl, mix soup, potato mix, cooked vegetables, thyme and pepper.

3 Unroll 1 can of dough; spread with half of soup mixture. Starting at shortest side, roll up; pinch edges to seal. Cut into 6 slices. Place 1 slice in each of 6 muffin cups. Repeat with remaining dough and soup mixture.

4 Bake 25 to 30 minutes or until golden brown. Brush top of each cupcake with melted butter; remove from pan. Serve immediately.

1 Serving: Calories 170; Total Fat 8g (Saturated Fat 3.5g, Trans Fat 0g); Cholesterol 5mg; Sodium 470mg; Total Carbohydrate 22g (Dietary Fiber 0g); Protein 3g **Exchanges:** 1 Starch, 1/2 Other Carbohydrate, 1 1/2 Fat **Carbohydrate Choices:** 1 1/2

tidbit

You can use 2 cans of refrigerated crescent rolls instead of the flaky dough sheets. If you substitute crescent rolls, be sure to firmly press the perforations to seal before spreading with the soup mixture.

rosemary-skewered meatball pops

PREP TIME: **40 Minutes** | START TO FINISH: **1 Hour 15 Minutes** | **60 meatball pops**

PASTA

- 9 oz uncooked linguine pasta
- ½ cup marinara sauce
- 1 egg, beaten
- ½ cup grated fresh Parmesan cheese

MEATBALLS

- 1 lb lean (at least 80%) ground beef
- ½ cup Italian-style bread crumbs
- ¼ cup milk
- ½ teaspoon finely chopped fresh rosemary
- ½ teaspoon Worcestershire sauce
- ½ teaspoon salt
- ¼ teaspoon pepper
- 1 small onion, finely chopped (⅓ cup)
- 1 egg

GARNISH AND ACCOMPANIMENTS

- 60 rosemary twigs or decorative skewers

  Additional marinara sauce, if desired

  Additional grated fresh Parmesan cheese, if desired

1 Heat oven to 400°F. Place mini paper baking cup in each of 60 mini muffin cups. Spray paper cups with cooking spray. Cook and drain linguine as directed on package using minimum cook time.

2 Meanwhile, in large bowl, mix meatball ingredients until well combined. Shape mixture into 60 (1-inch) meatballs.

3 In another large bowl, stir cooked linguine and remaining pasta ingredients. Wrap 3 to 4 linguine around 2 fingers; place around edge of each mini muffin cup. Place 1 meatball in center of pasta (linguine should form ring around meatball and meatball should touch bottom of paper cup).

4 Bake 11 to 14 minutes or until meatballs are thoroughly cooked and no longer pink in center.

5 To serve, remove each meatball with linguine from paper baking cup; insert rosemary sprig through linguine into meatball. Serve with additional marinara sauce and Parmesan cheese.

1 Meatball Pop: Calories 45; Total Fat 1.5g (Saturated Fat 0.5g, Trans Fat 0g); Cholesterol 10mg; Sodium 65mg; Total Carbohydrate 5g (Dietary Fiber 0g); Protein 2g **Exchanges:** ½ Starch **Carbohydrate Choices:** ½

tidbits

To make ahead, cook the linguine, shape the meatballs and arrange both in the muffin cups as directed. Cover with plastic wrap and refrigerate for up to 1 day or freeze for up to 2 weeks. To serve, remove from the refrigerator or freezer. Thaw if necessary and bake as directed adding an additional minute or two as needed to thoroughly cook the meatballs.

For evenly sized meatballs that will cook in the same amount of time, pat the meat mixture into a 10x6-inch rectangle. Cut into 60 (1-inch) squares. Roll each square into a ball.

30-minute mini meat loaves

PREP TIME: **10 Minutes** | START TO FINISH: **30 Minutes** | **6 servings (2 loaves each)**

½ cup ketchup

2 tablespoons packed brown sugar

1 lb lean (at least 80%) ground beef

½ lb ground pork

½ cup Original Bisquick mix

¼ teaspoon pepper

1 small onion, finely chopped (⅓ cup)

1 egg

1 Heat oven to 450°F. In small bowl, stir ketchup and brown sugar until mixed; reserve ¼ cup for topping. In large bowl, stir remaining ingredients and remaining ketchup mixture until well mixed.

2 Spray 13x9-inch pan with cooking spray. Place meat mixture in pan; pat into 12x4-inch rectangle. Cut lengthwise down center and then crosswise into sixths to form 12 loaves. Separate loaves, using spatula, so no edges are touching. Brush loaves with reserved ¼ cup ketchup mixture.

3 Bake 18 to 20 minutes or until loaves are no longer pink in center and meat thermometer inserted in center of loaves reads 160°F.

1 Serving: Calories 300; Total Fat 16g (Saturated Fat 6g, Trans Fat 1g); Cholesterol 105mg; Sodium 440mg; Total Carbohydrate 17g (Dietary Fiber 0g); Protein 22g **Exchanges:** 1 Starch, 3 Medium-Fat Meat, ½ Fat **Carbohydrate Choices:** 1

tidbits

While the mixture of ground beef and pork gives these little loaves a unique flavor, you can use 1½ pounds of ground beef instead of the mixture.

Serve these loaves alongside cooked baby-cut carrots and mashed potatoes. Apple or cherry crisp is a sweet way to end the meal.

spicy mini dogs

PREP TIME: **20 Minutes** | START TO FINISH: **20 Minutes** | **24 mini dogs**

1	package (9.25 oz) dinner rolls
1	tablespoon olive oil
24	miniature Cajun-style andouille sausages or cocktail-size smoked link sausages
¼	cup Creole mustard
¼	cup sweet pepper relish

1 Heat rolls as directed on package. Meanwhile, in 12-inch skillet, heat oil over medium heat. Cook sausages in oil 5 minutes, turning occasionally, until lightly browned and thoroughly heated.

2 Cut slit in top of each roll. Place 1 sausage in each roll; top with ½ teaspoon each mustard and relish.

1 Mini Dog: Calories 70; Total Fat 2.5g (Saturated Fat 0.5g, Trans Fat 0g); Cholesterol 10mg; Sodium 240mg; Total Carbohydrate 7g (Dietary Fiber 0g); Protein 3g **Exchanges:** ½ Starch, ½ Fat **Carbohydrate Choices:** ½

genoa salami stacks

PREP TIME: **20 Minutes** | START TO FINISH: **25 Minutes** | **24 servings**

24 slices (¼ to ½ inch thick) French baguette bread (from 10-oz loaf)

1½ cups finely shredded lettuce

¼ cup creamy Caesar dressing

6 thin slices (about ½ oz each) provolone cheese, cut into fourths

24 thin slices Genoa salami (4 oz), folded in half twice

4 plum (Roma) tomatoes, thinly sliced

¾ teaspoon garlic-pepper blend

⅓ cup shredded fresh basil leaves or chopped fresh parsley

1 Heat oven to 375°F. Place bread slices in ungreased 15x10x1-inch pan. Bake 5 to 7 minutes or until crisp; cool.

2 In small bowl, mix lettuce and dressing. Top each bread slice with lettuce mixture. Layer cheese, salami and tomatoes on bread. Sprinkle with garlic-pepper blend and basil.

1 Serving: Calories 60; Total Fat 4g (Saturated Fat 1.5g, Trans Fat 0g); Cholesterol 5mg; Sodium 180mg; Total Carbohydrate 4g (Dietary Fiber 0g); Protein 3g **Exchanges:** ½ Starch, ½ Fat **Carbohydrate Choices:** 0

tidbits

Lightly drizzle olive oil over the toasted bread instead of using the Caesar dressing.

Tuck fresh sprigs of oregano and basil among the salami stacks, and garnish with cherry tomatoes and olives.

shrimp and tomato martinis

PREP TIME: 20 Minutes | **START TO FINISH:** 20 Minutes | 8 servings

VINAIGRETTE

- ⅓ cup olive oil
- 2 tablespoons red wine vinegar
- 2 tablespoons sugar
- 1 teaspoon Dijon mustard
- 1 clove garlic, finely chopped

TOMATO RELISH

- 3 medium tomatoes, seeded, chopped (1½ cups)
- 2 cloves garlic, finely chopped
- 3 tablespoons chopped fresh basil leaves
- 2 tablespoons small capers, drained
- ½ teaspoon salt
- ½ teaspoon pepper

SHRIMP

- 24 medium cooked shrimp (thawed if frozen), peeled, deveined (tail shells removed)
- 8 fresh basil leaves, sliced

1 In small bowl, beat vinaigrette ingredients with whisk until smooth.

2 In medium bowl, mix tomato relish ingredients.

3 To serve, divide tomato relish evenly among 8 martini glasses. Top each with 3 shrimp. Spoon about 1 tablespoon vinaigrette over each. Garnish with sliced basil leaves.

1 Serving: Calories 120; Total Fat 9g (Saturated Fat 1.5g, Trans Fat 0g); Cholesterol 30mg; Sodium 260mg; Total Carbohydrate 5g (Dietary Fiber 0g); Protein 3g **Exchanges:** ½ Vegetable, ½ Very Lean Meat, 2 Fat **Carbohydrate Choices:** ½

tidbit

If you don't have martini glasses, use large wine glasses or lowball glasses.

fire-roasted crab shooters

PREP TIME: **15 Minutes** | START TO FINISH: **15 Minutes** | **8 servings**

1 can (14.5 oz) organic fire-roasted diced tomatoes, undrained

½ cup tomato juice

1 slice (¼ inch thick) red onion

1 tablespoon cider vinegar

1 tablespoon olive or vegetable oil

½ teaspoon salt

3 drops red pepper sauce

1 small cucumber, peeled, diced (¾ cup)

1 can (6½ oz) special white crabmeat, drained (about 1 cup)

2 teaspoons coarsely chopped fresh dill weed

1 In food processor, place all ingredients except cucumber, crabmeat and dill weed. Cover; process with on-and-off pulses until mixture is coarsely pureed. Stir in cucumber.

2 Spoon about ⅓ cup tomato mixture into each of 8 small glasses. Spoon about 1 heaping tablespoon crabmeat onto center of each cocktail. Sprinkle dill weed over top.

1 Serving: Calories 50; Total Fat 2g (Saturated Fat 0g, Trans Fat 0g); Cholesterol 15mg; Sodium 320mg; Total Carbohydrate 3g (Dietary Fiber 0g); Protein 4g **Exchanges:** ½ Other Carbohydrate, ½ Lean Meat **Carbohydrate Choices:** 0

tidbits

Canned crabmeat comes in different styles and varieties, including lump (most expensive), white and claw (least expensive). We chose the white for the best appearance in this elegant appetizer. Frozen crabmeat can be used instead of the canned, if desired.

Chill the tomato-cucumber mixture up to 1 hour before spooning into glasses. A bonus is the flavors will have blended more.

california sushi canapés

PREP TIME: 1 Hour 5 Minutes | START TO FINISH: **1 Hour 40 Minutes** | **16 servings (2 appetizers each)**

RICE

- 1 cup water
- ³⁄₄ cup uncooked sushi rice
- 2 tablespoons seasoned rice vinegar

SAUCE

- 3 tablespoons mayonnaise
- 2 teaspoons finely chopped gingerroot
- 1 teaspoon roasted red chili paste

CANAPÉS

- 1 small English (seedless) cucumber
- 1 sheet roasted seaweed nori sheets (8x7 inch; from 1-oz package), cut into 8 rows by 4 rows
- 2 tablespoons sesame seed, toasted*
- ½ avocado, pitted, peeled and cut lengthwise into thin slices
- ½ red bell pepper, finely chopped (or thinly sliced carrot or very small pieces of avocado)

1 In 1-quart saucepan, heat 1 cup water and the rice to boiling. Reduce heat to low. Cover; simmer 15 to 20 minutes or until tender. Spoon rice into large bowl, tossing rice with 2 forks to cool slightly. Gradually add vinegar, tossing constantly. Cover bowl with damp towel; cool rice about 45 minutes or until room temperature.

2 Meanwhile, in small bowl, stir together sauce ingredients. Cover; refrigerate until ready to assemble canapés.

3 Cut cucumber into 32 slices, each about ¼ inch thick. Arrange on serving platter. For each canapé, place 1 piece of nori on each cucumber slice. Top each with about ¼ teaspoon sauce. Scoop rice using 1 measuring teaspoon, pressing rice against side of bowl to pack into spoon and hold shape of spoon. Carefully remove rice from spoon; dip flat side into sesame seeds and place, flat side down, on sauce. If necessary, carefully reshape rice with fingers. Top with bell pepper or other toppings (or a combination). Serve immediately, or cover and refrigerate up to 2 hours.

*To toast the sesame seed, cook in skillet over medium-low heat 5 to 7 minutes, stirring frequently until browning begins, then stirring constantly until golden brown.

1 Serving: Calories 70; Total Fat 3g (Saturated Fat 0g, Trans Fat 0g); Cholesterol 0mg; Sodium 25mg; Total Carbohydrate 8g (Dietary Fiber 1g); Protein 1g **Exchanges:** ½ Starch, ½ Fat **Carbohydrate Choices:** ½

tidbits

Vary the vegetable toppings with sliced radishes, asparagus cuts or sliced green onions.

Seasoned rice vinegar contains salt and sugar to flavor the sushi. In this recipe, you can make your own from unseasoned rice vinegar by stirring in 2 teaspoons sugar and ¼ teaspoon salt.

basic cheese balls

PREP TIME: 1 Hour | START TO FINISH: 2 Hours 30 Minutes | 75 cheese balls

- 2 packages (8 oz each) cream cheese, softened
- 1 package (10 to 11 oz) chèvre (goat) cheese, softened
- 1 teaspoon fresh lemon juice
- ½ teaspoon Worcestershire sauce
- ¼ teaspoon kosher (coarse) salt
- ¼ teaspoon freshly ground black pepper

1 In large bowl, beat Basic Cheese Ball Ingredients (left) with electric mixer fitted with paddle attachment on medium speed until combined.

2 Stir in Flavor Stir-Ins for desired recipe (pages 107–109). With moistened hands, shape into 75 (1-inch) balls; refrigerate until firm, about 1 hour. (If not using immediately, cover and refrigerate up to 3 days, or freeze up to 1 month.

3 In small bowl, stir coating ingredients for desired recipe. Roll balls in mixture to coat before serving. Serve with baguette slices or as indicated in individual recipes.

Indian

Middle Eastern

Mexican

Korean

French

mini french cheese balls

BASIC CHEESE BALLS

FLAVOR STIR-INS

- 3 cups crumbled Roquefort cheese (12 oz)
- 2 tablespoons honey
- 3 tablespoons finely chopped shallot
- ¼ cup chopped fresh parsley

COATING

- ¾ cup chopped fresh parsley
- ¼ cup finely chopped Marcona almonds

SERVE-WITH, IF DESIRED

Toasted baguette slices

1 Cheese Ball: Calories 60; Total Fat 5g (Saturated Fat 3g, Trans Fat 0g); Cholesterol 15mg; Sodium 130mg; Total Carbohydrate 1g (Dietary Fiber 0g); Protein 2g **Exchanges**: ½ Medium-Fat Meat, ½ Fat **Carbohydrate Choices:** 0

mini korean cheese balls

BASIC CHEESE BALLS

FLAVOR STIR-INS

- 3 cups shredded mozzarella cheese (12 oz)
- 1½ teaspoons Korean chili paste
- ¾ cup finely chopped mild kimchi
- 6 tablespoons finely chopped green onions
- 1 tablespoon fresh grated lime peel

COATING

- 2¼ cups black sesame seed

SERVE-WITH, IF DESIRED

Rice crackers

1 Cheese Ball: Calories 80; Total Fat 7g (Saturated Fat 3g, Trans Fat 0g); Cholesterol 10mg; Sodium 90mg; Total Carbohydrate 1g (Dietary Fiber 0g); Protein 3g **Exchanges**: ½ Medium-Fat Meat, 1 Fat **Carbohydrate Choices:** 0

mini middle eastern cheese balls

BASIC CHEESE BALLS

FLAVOR STIR-INS

  3   cups crumbled feta cheese (12 oz)

  6   tablespoons chopped fresh mint leaves

1½ teaspoons za'atar seasoning blend

COATING

1½ teaspoons za'atar seasoning blend

1½ cups finely chopped pistachio nuts

SERVE-WITH, IF DESIRED

    Pita crackers

1 Cheese Ball: Calories 60 (Calories from Fat 50); Total Fat 5g (Saturated Fat 3g, Trans Fat 0g); Cholesterol 15mg; Sodium 90mg; Potassium 45mg; Total Carbohydrate 1g (Dietary Fiber 0g); Protein 2g **Exchanges:** ½ Medium-Fat Meat, ½ Fat **Carbohydrate Choices:** 0

mini mexican cheese balls

BASIC CHEESE BALLS

FLAVOR STIR-INS

  3   cups crumbled queso fresco cheese (12 oz)

1½ teaspoons ancho chile powder

  2   tablespoons chopped chipotle chiles in adobo sauce (from 7-oz can)

  6   tablespoons chopped green onions (6 medium)

COATING

1½ cups finely chopped pepitas (pumpkin seeds)

SERVE-WITH, IF DESIRED

    Tortilla chips

1 Cheese Ball: Calories 60; Total Fat 5g (Saturated Fat 2.5g, Trans Fat 0g); Cholesterol 15mg; Sodium 90mg; Total Carbohydrate 0g (Dietary Fiber 0g); Protein 2g **Exchanges:** ½ Medium-Fat Meat, ½ Fat **Carbohydrate Choices:** 0

mini indian cheese balls

BASIC CHEESE BALLS
FLAVOR STIR-INS

- 3 cups finely shredded paneer cheese (12 oz)
- 1 tablespoon fresh grated lime peel
- 1 tablespoon curry powder
- ¼ cup chopped fresh cilantro

COATING

- ¼ cup chopped fresh cilantro
- ¼ cup finely chopped roasted salted cashews

SERVE-WITH, IF DESIRED

- Naan bread

1 Cheese Ball: Calories 50; Total Fat 4.5g (Saturated Fat 2.5g, Trans Fat 0g); Cholesterol 10mg; Sodium 60mg; Total Carbohydrate 1g (Dietary Fiber 0g); Protein 2g **Exchanges:** ½ Medium-Fat Meat, ½ Fat **Carbohydrate Choices:** 0

tidbits

If not using immediately, shape the cheese balls, cover and refrigerate up to 3 days, or freeze up to 1 month. Allow cheese balls to thaw in the refrigerator before rolling in the coating and serving.

Some of the more unusual ingredients can be found in specialty stores and some large supermarkets.

For a party, it's fun to choose a couple of flavors of the cheese balls, and use part of the basic cheese ball mixture for each one.

mini tostada bites

16 restaurant-style tortilla chips

½ cup refrigerated guacamole

½ cup canned black beans, drained, rinsed

1 cup shredded deli rotisserie chicken (from 2-lb chicken)

3 tablespoons chopped fresh cilantro

Salsa, if desired

1 Place tortilla chips on serving platter. Top each chip with 1½ teaspoons guacamole, 1½ teaspoons beans and 1 tablespoon chicken. Sprinkle with cilantro.

2 Serve immediately, or cover and refrigerate up to 30 minutes before serving. Serve with salsa.

1 Bite: Calories 45; Total Fat 2g (Saturated Fat 0g, Trans Fat 0g); Cholesterol 10mg; Sodium 100mg; Total Carbohydrate 4g (Dietary Fiber 1g); Protein 3g **Exchanges:** ½ Starch, ½ Fat **Carbohydrate Choices:** 0

tidbit

To make Cajun-flavored bites, use Cajun-flavored rotisserie chicken to add an interesting kick to this recipe. Try other flavors of rotisserie chicken to change it up.

cheesy fig bites

PREP TIME: 30 Minutes | **START TO FINISH:** 30 Minutes | **30 bites**

2   packages (1.90 oz each) frozen mini fillo shells (30 shells total)

3   oz Brie cheese, cut into 60 (½-inch) cubes

⅓   cup green or red pepper jelly

10   dried Calimyrna figs, coarsely chopped (about ¾ cup)

¼   cup finely chopped pistachio nuts

2   tablespoons honey

1   tablespoon balsamic vinegar

1 Heat oven to 350°F. Place phyllo shells in ungreased 15x10x1-inch pan. Place 2 cubes of cheese into each shell. Bake 5 to 6 minutes or until shells are crisp and cheese is melted.

2 Meanwhile, in small microwavable bowl, microwave jelly on High 15 seconds or until drizzling consistency.

3 Spoon ½ teaspoon jelly and about 1 teaspoon chopped fig over cheese in each shell. Sprinkle each with about ¼ teaspoon pistachio nuts.

4 In small microwavable bowl, microwave honey on High 15 seconds or just until warm. Stir in vinegar; set aside to cool slightly. Drizzle each shell with about ¼ teaspoon honey-balsamic glaze.

1 Bite: Calories 60; Total Fat 2.5g (Saturated Fat 0.5g, Trans Fat 0g); Cholesterol 0mg; Sodium 30mg; Total Carbohydrate 8g (Dietary Fiber 0g); Protein 1g **Exchanges:** ½ Starch, ½ Fat **Carbohydrate Choices:** ½

tidbit

We like the Calimyrna figs because they're a sweeter variety, but any dried or fresh figs can be used in the recipe. For a pretty presentation, make half of the bites with Calimyrna and the other half with Mission figs.

potato salad bites

PREP TIME: **30 Minutes** | START TO FINISH: **2 Hours 20 Minutes** | **24 bites**

12 small red potatoes (1½ to 1¾ inches in diameter)

1 teaspoon salt

1 hard-cooked egg, finely chopped

¼ cup chopped celery

3 tablespoons dill pickle relish

2 tablespoons mayonnaise or salad dressing

1 teaspoon yellow mustard

¼ teaspoon pepper

2 medium green onions, thinly sliced (2 tablespoons)

3 radishes, thinly sliced (¼ cup), if desired

1 Heat oven to 400°F. Place potatoes in ungreased 15x10x1-inch pan. Bake 30 to 40 minutes or until tender. Cool 10 minutes or until cool enough to handle.

2 Cut potatoes in half. With melon baller, scoop out insides of potatoes into medium bowl, leaving ¼-inch lining of potato flesh around edges of shells. Sprinkle shells with ½ teaspoon of the salt. To potato flesh in bowl, add remaining ½ teaspoon salt and remaining ingredients except onions and radishes; mix well, breaking up potatoes.

3 Cut very thin slice off bottom of each potato shell so potatoes will stand upright. Fill each potato shell with about 1 tablespoon filling mixture. Top with onions. Cover; refrigerate about 1 hour or until chilled. Garnish with radish slices.

1 Bite: Calories 30; Total Fat 1g (Saturated Fat 0g, Trans Fat 0g); Cholesterol 10mg; Sodium 140mg; Total Carbohydrate 5g (Dietary Fiber 0g); Protein 0g **Exchanges:** ½ Other Carbohydrate **Carbohydrate Choices:** ½

tidbits

Purchasing already cooked eggs is a real time-saver. They're usually found in the deli or dairy department of the grocery store.

A small teaspoon can be used to scoop out the potatoes if a melon baller is not available. A small cookie scoop works well for filling the potato shells.

peach and cheesy caprese bites

PREP TIME: **30 Minutes** | START TO FINISH: **1 Hour** | **24 bites**

¼   cup olive oil

2   teaspoons grated lemon peel

2   tablespoons fresh lemon juice

½   cup coarsely chopped fresh basil leaves

½   teaspoon salt

¼   teaspoon freshly ground black pepper

½   English cucumber, unpeeled

1   large peach or nectarine, cut into 24 (½-inch) pieces

24   fresh mozzarella cheese balls (from 8-oz container), drained

24   fresh basil leaves (about 2 oz)

24   toothpicks or short skewers

1 In large bowl, mix oil, lemon peel, lemon juice, chopped basil, salt and pepper with whisk until blended.

2 Cut cucumber into 12 (½-inch) slices; cut each crosswise in half to make 24 pieces. Add cucumbers, peach pieces and cheese to oil mixture; toss to coat. Cover; refrigerate about 30 minutes.

3 Drain cucumber mixture. Thread cucumber, peach, basil and cheese alternately onto toothpicks.

1 Bite: Calories 50; Total Fat 4g (Saturated Fat 1.5g, Trans Fat 0g); Cholesterol 5mg; Sodium 80mg; Total Carbohydrate 1g (Dietary Fiber 0g); Protein 1g **Exchanges:** 1 Fat **Carbohydrate Choices:** 0

tidbit

For a pretty display on your platter, use a variety of frilly skewers or picks to make the bites. Then garnish the presentation with more basil and lemon curls.

veggie strips with sriracha hummus

PREP TIME: 30 Minutes | **START TO FINISH:** 30 Minutes | **12 servings**

SRIRACHA HUMMUS

- 1 cup plain hummus (from 10-oz container)
- ⅓ cup coarsely chopped, well drained roasted red peppers (from 16-oz jar)
- 1 tablespoon Sriracha sauce

VEGETABLES

- 12 Bibb lettuce leaves
- 1 medium carrot, cut into 2x¼-inch strips (¾ cup)
- 1 small red bell pepper, cut into 2x¼-inch strips (about ¾ cup)
- 1 baby seedless cucumber, cut into 2x¼-inch strips (¾ cup)
- ½ small jicama, peeled, cut into 2x¼-inch strips (¾ cup)

1 In food processor, process sriracha hummus ingredients until smooth.

2 Spoon about 2 tablespoons hummus into bottom of each of 12 shot glasses (about 3 oz) or small serving glasses.

3 Fold each lettuce leaf; place 1 against side of each shot glass, slightly sticking into hummus. Add equal amounts of carrot, bell pepper, cucumber and jicama to each shot glass. Serve immediately, or refrigerate up to 3 hours before serving.

1 Serving: Calories 50; Total Fat 2g (Saturated Fat 0g, Trans Fat 0g); Cholesterol 0mg; Sodium 120mg; Total Carbohydrate 7g (Dietary Fiber 2g); Protein 2g **Exchanges:** ½ Other Carbohydrate, ½ Vegetable, ½ Fat **Carbohydrate Choices:** ½

tidbit

Sriracha is a wonderful spicy sauce that adds some heat to the hummus dip in this recipe. Go ahead and taste before you spoon into the glasses—add a few drops more if you like it spicier!

mini 7-layer dips

PREP TIME: **30 Minutes** | START TO FINISH: **30 Minutes** | **10 servings**

1 can (16 oz) refried beans

2 tablespoons taco seasoning mix (from 1-oz package)

1 container (8 oz) sour cream

1 can (4.5 oz) chopped green chiles, drained

1¼ cups guacamole

1¼ cups chunky-style salsa (from 16-oz jar)

1 cup shredded Cheddar or Colby–Monterey Jack cheese blend (4 oz)

1 cup shredded lettuce

2 tablespoons sliced ripe olives

1 In small bowl, mix refried beans and 2 tablespoons taco seasoning mix. Spread about 3 tablespoons mixture in bottom of each of ten 6-oz custard cups or 9-oz clear plastic cups.

2 Mix sour cream and green chiles; divide evenly among cups (about 2 tablespoons per cup). Top each with about 2 tablespoons each guacamole and salsa, slightly less than 1 tablespoon each cheese and lettuce, and a few olive slices.

1 Serving: Calories 170; Total Fat 10g (Saturated Fat 5g, Trans Fat 0g); Cholesterol 25mg; Sodium 810mg; Total Carbohydrate 13g (Dietary Fiber 3g); Protein 6g **Exchanges:** 1 Starch, 2 Fat **Carbohydrate Choices:** 1

tidbits

You will not need the entire package of taco seasoning, so save the remaining seasoning mix for another use. Try sprinkling chicken or pork with the seasoning before grilling.

This dip is delicious with veggies dipped in it as well; try celery, carrots, jicama, etc.

sweet shots and pops

Add a sweet note to any bash with these charming handheld desserts—they taste as great as they look!

dark chocolate–raspberry trifle shooters

PREP TIME: **15 Minutes** | START TO FINISH: **35 Minutes** | **8 servings**

⅔ cup whipping cream

1 cup dark chocolate chips (6 oz)

½ cup shortbread cookie crumbs

¼ cup seedless red raspberry preserves

2 teaspoons orange-flavored liqueur

32 fresh raspberries

8 orange curls, if desired for garnish

1 shortbread cookie, cut into 8 small wedges

1 In 1-quart saucepan, heat whipping cream over medium heat, stirring occasionally, just until cream begins to simmer (do not boil). Remove from heat. With whisk, stir in chocolate chips until melted and smooth. Remove from heat; let stand 5 minutes.

2 Meanwhile, spoon 1 tablespoon cookie crumbs into bottom of each of 8 (3-oz) shot glasses or other small glasses. Press crumbs gently with back of spoon to level.

3 Carefully spoon 2 tablespoons cooled chocolate mixture over crumbs in each glass. Refrigerate 20 minutes or until set.

4 In small bowl, beat preserves and liqueur with fork until smooth. Place 3 raspberries over chocolate in each cup. Spoon 1 heaping teaspoon preserves mixture over raspberries. Top each with 1 raspberry. Garnish each with orange curl and cookie wedge.

1 Serving: Calories 280; Total Fat 17g (Saturated Fat 9g, Trans Fat 1g); Cholesterol 30mg; Sodium 70mg; Total Carbohydrate 29g (Dietary Fiber 2g); Protein 2g **Carbohydrate Choices:** 2

tidbit

To make orange curls for garnishing this pretty dessert, use a vegetable peeler to remove strips of peel from an orange. Then curl the strips with your fingers and place on the desserts.

cheesecake shot glass desserts

PREP TIME: 30 Minutes | **START TO FINISH: 1 Hour** | **12 servings**

2 packages (8 oz each) cream cheese, softened

¾ cup sugar

4 teaspoons grated lemon peel

¼ cup graham cracker crumbs

Fresh blueberries and raspberries

1 In large bowl, beat cream cheese and sugar with electric mixer on medium speed until smooth. Stir in lemon peel.

2 Spoon 2 teaspoons graham cracker crumbs into bottoms of 12 (2-oz) cordial glasses (shot glasses). Top each with 2 tablespoons lemon cream cheese mixture. Sprinkle with 2 teaspoons graham cracker crumbs and another 2 tablespoons lemon cream cheese mixture. Top with berries. Refrigerate at least 30 minutes before serving.

1 Serving: Calories 210; Total Fat 14g (Saturated Fat 8g, Trans Fat 0g); Cholesterol 40mg; Sodium 150mg; Total Carbohydrate 19g (Dietary Fiber 0g); Protein 2g **Exchanges:** 1 Starch, ½ Other Carbohydrate, 2½ Fat **Carbohydrate Choices:** 1

tidbits

For a rich chocolate variation, substitute 2 tablespoons coffee-flavored liqueur or 2 teaspoons chocolate extract for the lemon peel, chocolate cookie crumbs for the graham cracker crumbs, and grated chocolate for the berries.

This is a great opportunity to use any souvenir shot glasses you have on hand. Or, use 2 oz plastic cups, available in party supply stores.

strawberry mousse dessert cups

PREP TIME: **25 Minutes** | START TO FINISH: **1 Hour 25 Minutes** | **24 servings**

½ teaspoon unflavored gelatin
1 tablespoon whipping cream
1 cup sliced fresh strawberries
½ cup powdered sugar
½ cup whipping cream
½ teaspoon vanilla
24 miniature dessert or cordial chocolate cups
Additional sliced fresh strawberries, if desired

1 In small bowl, sprinkle gelatin over 1 tablespoon whipping cream; set aside to soften gelatin.

2 Place strawberries and powdered sugar in food processor. Cover; process until smooth. Pour mixture into 1-quart saucepan; add softened gelatin. Cook over medium heat, beating with whisk occasionally, until mixture comes to a simmer and gelatin is dissolved. Remove from heat; cool 30 minutes.

3 In small bowl, beat ½ cup whipping cream and the vanilla with electric mixer on high speed until stiff peaks form. On low speed, beat strawberry mixture into whipped cream until blended.

4 Place mousse in decorating bag fitted with small star tip. Pipe mousse into chocolate cups. Refrigerate until set, about 30 minutes, or up to 2 hours before serving. Garnish with additional sliced strawberries.

1 Serving: Calories 50; Total Fat 3g (Saturated Fat 2g, Trans Fat 0g); Cholesterol 5mg; Sodium 0mg; Total Carbohydrate 6g (Dietary Fiber 0g); Protein 0g **Exchanges:** ½ Other Carbohydrate, ½ Fat **Carbohydrate Choices:** ½

tidbit

If the chocolate cups are unavailable, you can make your own by painting the inside of mini paper cups with melted chocolate or confectionary chocolate. Let the caps stand until set.

lemon dessert shots

PREP TIME: 30 Minutes | **START TO FINISH: 1 Hour** | **12 servings**

10 gingersnap cookies

2 oz ⅓-less-fat cream cheese (Neufchâtel), softened

½ cup marshmallow creme (from 7-oz jar)

1 container (6 oz) honey vanilla fat-free Greek yogurt

½ cup lemon curd (from 10-oz jar)

36 fresh raspberries

½ cup frozen (thawed) reduced-fat whipped topping

1 In 1-quart resealable food-storage plastic bag, place cookies; seal bag. Crush with rolling pin; place in small bowl.

2 In medium bowl, beat cream cheese and marshmallow creme with electric mixer on low speed until smooth. Beat in yogurt until blended. Place mixture in 1-quart resealable food-storage plastic bag; seal bag. In 1-pint resealable food-storage plastic bag, place lemon curd; seal bag. Cut ⅛-inch opening diagonally across bottom corner of each bag.

3 In bottom of each of 12 (2-oz) shot glasses, place 1 raspberry. Pipe about 2 teaspoons yogurt mixture over raspberry in each glass. Pipe ¼-inch ring of lemon curd around edge of glass; sprinkle with about 1 teaspoon cookies. Repeat.

4 Garnish each dessert shot with dollop of about 2 teaspoons whipped topping and 1 raspberry. Place in 9-inch square pan. Refrigerate about 30 minutes or until chilled, but no longer than 3 hours.

1 Serving: Calories 110; Total Fat 3g (Saturated Fat 1.5g, Trans Fat 0g); Cholesterol 15mg; Sodium 70mg; Total Carbohydrate 18g (Dietary Fiber 0g); Protein 2g **Exchanges:** ½ Starch, ½ Other Carbohydrate, ½ Fat **Carbohydrate Choices:** 1

tidbit

Shot glasses often have some kind of writing on them. For a prettier presentation, purchase plain, plastic shot glasses at your local party store or online.

cake and ice cream shots

PREP TIME: 20 Minutes | **START TO FINISH: 1 Hour 40 Minutes** | **24 servings**

1 box yellow cake mix with pudding

Water, vegetable oil and eggs called for on cake mix box

1 quart (4 cups) strawberry ice cream

24 creme-filled chocolate sandwich cookies, chopped

2 cups whipped cream topping (from aerosol can)

1 Heat oven to 350°F (325°F for dark or nonstick pan). Spray 13x9-inch pan with baking spray with flour.

2 Bake and cool cake as directed on box for 13x9-inch pan. Crumble cake with fork.

3 In each of 24 (4-oz) glass jars or cups, place 1 small scoop of ice cream. Layer with crumbled cake and half of the cookie pieces. Top with remaining ice cream, the whipped topping and remaining cookie pieces. Serve immediately, or cover and freeze up to 4 hours.

1 Serving: Calories 230; Total Fat 12g (Saturated Fat 4g, Trans Fat 0g); Cholesterol 35mg; Sodium 210mg; Total Carbohydrate 29g (Dietary Fiber 0g); Protein 2g **Exchanges:** 2 Other Carbohydrate, 2½ Fat **Carbohydrate Choices:** 2

tidbits

This recipe was developed by bloggers Adam and Joanne Gallagher from Inspired Taste.

Make these shooters up to 4 hours ahead of time; just keep them covered in the freezer until you're ready to serve.

Small canning jars or jelly jars work great for these shooters. For a special touch, place them in colorful paper baking cups when serving.

pomegranate–tequila sunrise jelly shots

PREP TIME: **30 Minutes** | START TO FINISH: **4 Hours** | **12 servings**

¾ cup pulp-free orange juice

2 envelopes unflavored gelatin

6 tablespoons silver or gold tequila

½ cup 100% pomegranate juice

¼ cup sugar

¼ cup water

Orange slices, if desired

1 Lightly spray 12 (2-oz) shot glasses with cooking spray; gently wipe any excess with paper towel. Pour orange juice into 1-quart saucepan; sprinkle 1 envelope gelatin evenly over juice to soften. Heat over low heat, stirring constantly, until gelatin is completely dissolved; remove from heat. Stir in tequila.

2 Divide orange juice mixture evenly among shot glasses (about 2 tablespoons per glass). Place shot glasses in 9-inch square pan. Refrigerate about 30 minutes or until almost set. (Setting the first layer helps to give the 2-layer appearance and also ensures the desserts will release from the glasses in 1 piece, rather than 2 separate layers.)

3 Meanwhile, in same saucepan, stir pomegranate juice, sugar and water. Sprinkle remaining 1 envelope gelatin evenly over juice to soften. Heat over low heat, stirring constantly, until gelatin is completely dissolved; remove from heat.

4 Remove shot glasses from refrigerator (orange layer should appear mostly set). Pour pomegranate mixture evenly over top of orange layer in glasses (about 4 teaspoons per glass). Refrigerate at least 3 hours until completely chilled and firm.

5 Just before serving, dip a table knife into hot water; slide knife along inside edge of shot glass to loosen. Shake jelly shot out of glass onto plate (or serve from glass with a spoon); repeat with remaining jelly shots. Serve jelly shot on orange slice.

1 Serving: Calories 50; Total Fat 0g (Saturated Fat 0g, Trans Fat 0g); Cholesterol 0mg; Sodium 0mg; Total Carbohydrate 7g (Dietary Fiber 0g); Protein 1g **Exchanges:** ½ Starch **Carbohydrate Choices:** ½

stout beer and ice cream mini floats

PREP TIME: **5 Minutes** | START TO FINISH: **5 Minutes** | **8 servings**

1 cup vanilla ice cream

½ cup stout draught beer (from 14.9-oz can)

3 tablespoons chocolate-flavor syrup

1 Using small ice cream scoop (about 1 tablespoon each), place 2 small scoops ice cream in each of 8 shot glasses. Slowly pour about 1 tablespoon beer into each glass.

2 Drizzle each with about 1 teaspoon chocolate syrup. Serve immediately with small spoons.

1 Serving: Calories 100; Total Fat 5g (Saturated Fat 3g, Trans Fat 0g); Cholesterol 30mg; Sodium 20mg; Total Carbohydrate 13g (Dietary Fiber 0g); Protein 1g **Exchanges:** 1 Other Carbohydrate, 1 Fat **Carbohydrate Choices:** 1

black and tan beer pops

PREP TIME: 40 Minutes | **START TO FINISH: 11 Hours 40 Minutes** | **14 pops**

TAN LAYER

- ½ can (14-oz size) sweetened condensed milk (⅔ cup)
- ¼ cup cold brown ale beer
- 1½ teaspoons vanilla
- 1 cup whipping cream
- 14 paper cups (5-oz size)
- 14 craft sticks (flat wooden sticks with round ends)

BLACK LAYER

- ½ can (14-oz size) sweetened condensed milk (⅔ cup)
- ¼ cup cold stout beer
- 2 tablespoons chocolate-flavor syrup
- 1½ teaspoons vanilla
- 1 cup whipping cream

1 In medium bowl, stir together ⅔ cup condensed milk, the brown ale beer and 1½ teaspoons vanilla until well mixed. In chilled medium bowl, beat 1 cup whipping cream with electric mixer on high speed until stiff peaks form. Fold whipped cream into condensed milk mixture. Divide mixture among paper cups (about ¼ cup each). Cover with foil; insert craft stick through foil into center of pop. Freeze 3 to 4 hours or until frozen.

2 When first layer is frozen, make black layer. In medium bowl, stir together ⅔ cup condensed milk, the stout beer, chocolate syrup and 1½ teaspoons vanilla until well mixed. In chilled medium bowl, beat 1 cup whipping cream with electric mixer on high speed until stiff peaks form. Fold whipped cream into condensed milk mixture.

3 Remove foil from pops. Pour black layer mixture over frozen tan layer. Return foil to pops to help support sticks. Freeze about 8 hours or until frozen. Store remaining pops covered in freezer.

1 Pop: Calories 210; Total Fat 13g (Saturated Fat 8g, Trans Fat 0g); Cholesterol 50mg; Sodium 50mg; Total Carbohydrate 19g (Dietary Fiber 0g); Protein 3g **Exchanges:** 1 Starch, 2½ Fat **Carbohydrate Choices:** 1

tidbit

Be sure to allow the tan layer to freeze completely before adding the black layer.

piña colada cake pops

PREP TIME: 30 Minutes | **START TO FINISH:** 30 Minutes | 24 cake pops

2 (10-inch) angel food cakes

1 container (6 oz) light piña colada yogurt

2 oz (from 8-oz package) 1/3-less-fat cream cheese (Neufchâtel), softened

2 tablespoons powdered sugar

24 paper lollipop sticks

Candy sprinkles or shredded coconut, if desired

1 Break up angel food cake into small pieces and place in food processor. Cover; process with on-and-off pulses in batches until crumbs form. Do not over process (to avoid cake sticking). Place in large bowl.

2 In medium bowl, stir yogurt, cream cheese and powdered sugar until smooth. Pour into cake crumb bowl. Mix well. Shape mixture into 24 golf ball–size pops, about 2 tablespoons each. Poke lollipop stick into each pop. Roll pops in sprinkles. Refrigerate.

1 Cake Pop: Calories 140; Total Fat 0g (Saturated Fat 0g, Trans Fat 0g); Cholesterol 0mg; Sodium 390mg; Total Carbohydrate 30g (Dietary Fiber 0g); Protein 4g **Exchanges:** 1½ Starch, ½ Other Carbohydrate **Carbohydrate Choices:** 2

tidbit

For ease in shaping the cake pops, use a #24 scoop to measure.

tequila sunrise cake pops

PREP TIME: **1 Hour 5 Minutes** | START TO FINISH: **3 Hours 10 Minutes** | **18 cake pops**

CAKE

1	cup all-purpose flour
1/3	cup granulated sugar
1	tablespoon grated orange peel
1	teaspoon baking powder
1/4	teaspoon baking soda
1/4	teaspoon salt
1/4	cup orange juice
1/4	cup vegetable oil
2	tablespoons orange-flavored liqueur
1	tablespoon grenadine syrup
2	eggs

FILLING

1/4	cup butter, softened
1½	cups powdered sugar
3	tablespoons tequila

COATING

1	bag (12 oz) yellow candy melts
28	paper lollipop sticks (6 inch)
2	blocks white plastic foam (each about 12x3x2 inches)
1	bag (12 oz) orange candy melts
	Red colored sugar

1 Heat oven to 350°F (325°F for dark or nonstick pan). Spray bottom of 8x4-inch loaf pan with cooking spray. In large bowl, beat cake ingredients with electric mixer on low speed until mixed, then on medium speed 2 minutes. Pour into pan.

2 Bake 30 to 35 minutes or until toothpick inserted in center comes out clean. Cool in pan 10 minutes; remove to cooling rack. Cool completely, about 50 minutes. Trim browned edges from sides and bottom of cake.

3 In food processor with metal blade, crumble half of cake. Cover; process with on-and-off pulses until cake is fine crumbs. Place in large bowl; repeat with remaining cake.

4 In small bowl, beat filling ingredients on low speed until mixed, then on medium speed until creamy. Add to cake crumbs, and mix until all crumbs are moistened and mixture holds together. Shape into 18 (1½-inch) balls; place on waxed paper–lined cookie sheet. Freeze 30 minutes.

5 In 2-cup microwavable measuring cup, microwave yellow candy melts as directed on package until melted. Remove several cake balls from freezer at a time. Dip top ½ inch of each lollipop stick into melted coating, and insert 1 inch into each cake ball. Dip into melted candy to cover; very gently tap off excess. (Reheat candy in microwave or add vegetable oil if too thick to coat.) Poke opposite end of stick into foam block. Let stand until set.

6 In another 2-cup microwavable measuring cup, microwave orange candy melts as directed on package until melted. Dip bottom half of each yellow-coated cake pop into orange melted candy. Dip tops into red colored sugar. Place in foam block. Let stand until set.

1 Cake Pop: Calories 370; Total Fat 18g (Saturated Fat 13g, Trans Fat 0g); Cholesterol 30mg; Sodium 150mg; Total Carbohydrate 47g (Dietary Fiber 0g); Protein 2g **Exchanges:** 1 Starch, 2 Other Carbohydrate, 3½ Fat **Carbohydrate Choices:** 3

tidbits

The cake pops are actually better the second day, as the flavors have a chance to mellow. They will keep at room temperature for several days.

You can find the candy melts at your local craft store, in the candy-making and cake-decorating section.

strawberries and cream cake pops

PREP TIME: **40 Minutes** | START TO FINISH: **2 Hours 10 Minutes** | **36 cake pops**

1 box white cake mix with pudding

Water, vegetable oil and egg whites called for on cake mix box

½ cup powdered sugar

2 oz cream cheese, softened

¼ cup butter, softened

¼ cup strawberry jam

1 cup dried strawberries, chopped

1 cup red candy melts (from 14-oz bag), melted

2 bags (14 oz each) pink candy melts or coating wafers, melted

36 paper lollipop sticks

1 large block white plastic foam

½ cup pink sugar

1 Heat oven to 350°F (325°F for dark or nonstick pan). Bake cake as directed on box for 13x9-inch pan, using water, vegetable oil and egg whites. Cool completely, about 1 hour.

2 Line cookie sheet with waxed paper. In large bowl, beat powdered sugar, cream cheese, butter and jam with electric mixer on medium speed until blended. Crumble cake into cream cheese mixture; mix well. Stir in dried strawberries. Shape into 36 (2-inch) balls; place on cookie sheet. Freeze until firm; transfer to refrigerator.

3 Spoon about 2 tablespoons melted red candy into pink candy; swirl gently. Remove several cake balls from refrigerator at a time. Dip tip of 1 lollipop stick about ½ inch into melted candy, and insert stick into 1 cake ball no more than halfway. Dip each cake ball into swirled candy to cover; tap off excess. (Spoon more red candy into pink candy as needed.) Poke opposite end of stick into foam block. Sprinkle with pink sugar. Let stand until set.

1 Cake Pop: Calories 278; Total Fat 13g (Saturated Fat 7g); Sodium 118mg; Total Carbohydrate 40g (Dietary Fiber 0g); Protein 1g **Exchanges:** ½ Starch, 2 Other Carbohydrate, 2½ Fat **Carbohydrate Choices:** 2½

candy corn cake pops

PREP TIME: **1 Hour 30 Minutes** | START TO FINISH: **3 Hours** | **72 cake pops**

1 box yellow cake mix with pudding

Water, vegetable oil and eggs called for on cake mix box

1 cup whipped fluffy white ready-to-spread frosting (from 12-oz container)

5 cups yellow candy melts

¼ cup shortening

2 cups orange candy melts

1 cup white candy melts

72 paper lollipop sticks

1 large block white plastic foam

1 Make and bake cake mix as directed on box for 13x9-inch pan, using water, oil and eggs. Cool. Line cookie sheet with waxed paper. Crumble cake into large bowl. Add frosting; mix well. Roll into 72 (1-inch) balls; shape each ball into triangle, pressing sides flat to look like candy corn. Place on cookie sheet. Freeze until firm. Keep refrigerated.

2 In microwavable bowl, microwave yellow candy melts and 2 tablespoons of the shortening uncovered on Medium (50%) 1 minute, then in 15-second intervals, until melted; stir until smooth. Repeat with orange candy melts and white candy melts, using 1 tablespoon shortening for each. Dip tip of 1 lollipop stick about ½ inch into melted yellow candy and insert stick into base of 1 cake triangle no more than halfway. Repeat. Return to cookie sheet. Refrigerate 5 minutes.

3 Remove from refrigerator a few at a time. Dip cake triangles in melted yellow candy; tap off excess. Poke opposite end of stick into foam block. Let stand until set. Dip two-thirds of each cake triangle into melted orange candy; let stand until set. Dip tips in melted white candy; let stand until set.

1 Cake Pop: Calories 160; Total Fat 9g (Saturated Fat 6g, Trans Fat 0g); Cholesterol 10mg; Sodium 70mg; Total Carbohydrate 19g (Dietary Fiber 0g); Protein 1g **Exchanges:** 1 Other Carbohydrate, 2 Fat **Carbohydrate Choices:** 1

boston cream cake pops

PREP TIME: **50 Minutes** | START TO FINISH: **3 Hours 35 Minutes** | **24 cake pops**

1   box yellow cake mix with pudding

Water, vegetable oil and eggs called for on cake mix box

3   tablespoons sugar

1   tablespoon cornstarch

Dash salt

1   cup milk

2   egg yolks, beaten

1   tablespoon butter

½   teaspoon vanilla or vanilla bean paste

24   paper lollipop sticks

1   package (16 oz) chocolate-flavored candy coating, chopped, melted

1   large block white plastic foam

½   cup white vanilla baking chips

½   teaspoon shortening

1   Heat oven to 350°F. Spray bottom of 13x9-inch pan with cooking spray. Make and bake cake mix in pan as directed on box, using water, oil and eggs. Cool.

2   In 2-quart saucepan, mix sugar, cornstarch and salt. Add milk and egg yolks. Cook and stir over medium heat until mixture boils. Boil 1 minute. Stir in butter and vanilla. Remove from heat. Cover surface of pudding with plastic wrap; cool.

3   Line cookie sheet with waxed paper. Crumble cake into large bowl. Add pudding; mix well with fingers until mixture comes together. Shape into 24 (1½-inch) balls; place on cookie sheet. Freeze until firm; transfer to refrigerator.

4   Remove cake balls from refrigerator a few at a time. Dip tip of 1 lollipop stick about ½ inch into melted candy and insert stick no more than halfway into 1 cake ball. Dip each cake ball into melted candy to cover; tap off excess. Poke opposite end of stick into foam block. Let stand until set. In microwave, melt baking chips with shortening; drizzle over pops. Let stand until set.

1 Cake Pop: Calories 270; Total Fat 15g (Saturated Fat 9g, Trans Fat 0g); Cholesterol 30mg; Sodium 190mg; Total Carbohydrate 33g (Dietary Fiber 0g); Protein 2g **Exchanges:** 1 Starch, 1 Other Carbohydrate, 3 Fat **Carbohydrate Choices:** 2

cappuccino cake pops

PREP TIME: 1 Hour 40 Minutes | **START TO FINISH:** 3 Hours 45 Minutes | 50 cake pops

½ cup hot water

6 tablespoons instant espresso coffee powder or granules

1 cup plus 2 tablespoons all-purpose flour

½ teaspoon baking soda

¼ teaspoon salt

⅔ cup sugar

¼ cup butter, softened

2 eggs

2 tablespoons coffee-flavored liqueur

¼ cup buttermilk

2 containers (12 oz each) milk chocolate whipped ready-to-spread frosting

50 paper lollipop sticks

2 blocks white plastic foam

½ cup fluffy white whipped ready-to-spread frosting (from 12-oz container)

50 chocolate-covered coffee beans (about 1 cup)

2 tablespoons unsweetened baking cocoa

1 Heat oven to 350°F. Grease bottom and sides of 8-inch square pan with shortening; lightly flour. In small bowl, stir hot water and coffee powder until coffee is dissolved; set aside. In medium bowl, mix flour, baking soda and salt; set aside.

2 In large bowl, beat sugar and butter with electric mixer on medium speed until light and fluffy. Beat in eggs, one at a time, just until blended. Beat in liqueur and coffee mixture. On low speed, alternately add flour mixture and buttermilk, beating just until blended after each addition. Pour into pan.

3 Bake 28 to 30 minutes or until toothpick inserted in center comes out clean. Cool 10 minutes; remove from pan to cooling rack. Cool completely, about 45 minutes.

4 Line cookie sheet with waxed paper. With fingers, crumble cake into large bowl. Add ½ cup of the chocolate frosting; mix well with spoon. Roll cake mixture into 50 (1-inch) balls; place on cookie sheet. Freeze about 30 minutes or until firm; transfer to refrigerator.

5 In medium microwavable bowl, microwave remaining chocolate frosting uncovered on Medium (50%) 30 seconds or until melted; stir until smooth. Remove several cake balls from refrigerator at a time. For each pop, dip tip of 1 lollipop stick about ½ inch into melted frosting, and insert stick into 1 cake ball no more than halfway. Dip cake ball into melted frosting to cover; tap off any excess. Poke opposite end of stick into foam block. Let stand until set.

6 In small microwavable bowl, microwave white frosting uncovered on Medium (50%) 10 to 20 seconds or until melted; stir until smooth. Spoon ½ teaspoon frosting on top of each cake pop, letting it drip down sides slightly. Immediately top with coffee bean. Let stand until set. Sprinkle lightly with cocoa. Store loosely covered in refrigerator.

1 Cake Pop: Calories 120; Total Fat 5g (Saturated Fat 2g, Trans Fat 0.5g); Cholesterol 10mg; Sodium 70mg; Total Carbohydrate 16g (Dietary Fiber 0g); Protein 1g **Exchanges:** 1 Other Carbohydrate, 1 Fat **Carbohydrate Choices:** 1

trix cereal cake pops

PREP TIME: 1 Hour 15 Minutes | START TO FINISH: **5 Hours 45 Minutes** | **48 cake pops**

1 box yellow or white cake mix with pudding

Water, vegetable oil and eggs or egg whites called for on cake mix box

1 container (1 lb) vanilla creamy ready-to-spread frosting

4 cups Trix™ cereal

36 oz vanilla-flavored candy coating (almond bark)

48 paper lollipop sticks

1 Heat oven to 350°F (325°F for dark or nonstick pan). Bake cake as directed on box for 13x9-inch pan. Cool completely, about 1 hour.

2 In large bowl, crumble cake; stir in frosting until well blended. Refrigerate about 2 hours or until firm enough to shape.

3 Roll cake mixture into 48 (1½-inch) balls; place on cookie sheet. Freeze 1 to 2 hours or until firm. Meanwhile, coarsely crush cereal. Line cookie sheet with waxed paper.

4 In 1-quart microwavable bowl, microwave 12 oz of the candy coating uncovered on High 1 minute 30 seconds; stir. Continue microwaving and stirring in 15-second intervals until melted; stir until smooth. Remove one-third of the balls from freezer. Using 2 forks, dip and roll each ball in coating. Place on waxed paper–lined cookie sheet. Immediately sprinkle with crushed cereal. Melt remaining candy coating in 12-oz batches; dip remaining balls, and sprinkle with cereal. Place in refrigerator.

5 To serve, carefully insert sticks into cake balls. Store any remaining cake balls in airtight container in refrigerator.

1 Cake Pop: Calories 220; Total Fat 11g (Saturated Fat 5g, Trans Fat 0.5g); Cholesterol 20mg; Sodium 125mg; Total Carbohydrate 29g (Dietary Fiber 0g); Protein 2g **Exchanges:** 1 Starch, 1 Other Carbohydrate, 2 Fat **Carbohydrate Choices:** 2

tidbit

For a fun display, insert cake pop sticks into a foam block.

strawberry-rhubarb pie pops

PREP TIME: **30 Minutes** | START TO FINISH: **1 Hour 25 Minutes** | **8 pie pops**

¾ cup frozen strawberries, thawed, chopped, drained and juice reserved

⅓ cup granulated sugar

2 teaspoons cornstarch

1 cup frozen chopped rhubarb, thawed

1 box refrigerated pie crusts, softened as directed on box

8 craft sticks (flat wooden sticks with round ends)

1 egg white, beaten

1 teaspoon granulated sugar

⅓ cup powdered sugar, if desired

2 to 3 teaspoons milk, if desired

1 Heat oven to 450°F. In medium bowl, place reserved strawberry juice. In small bowl, mix ⅓ cup granulated sugar and the cornstarch. Add to strawberry juice, beating with whisk. Stir in strawberries and rhubarb.

2 Unroll pie crusts on work surface. Using 3½-inch round cutter, cut 8 rounds from each crust. Place 8 rounds on ungreased cookie sheet. Spoon fruit mixture evenly on each round to within ½ inch of edge. Place 1 craft stick in filling on each round.

3 Flatten remaining rounds to 4-inch diameter. Brush underside of rounds with egg white; place over fruit. Press edges together; seal with fork. Cut small slits in tops of pies. Brush tops with egg white; sprinkle evenly with 1 teaspoon granulated sugar.

4 Bake 10 to 13 minutes or until golden brown. Remove from cookie sheet to cooling rack; cool 10 minutes.

5 In small bowl, mix powdered sugar and enough milk until glaze is smooth and thin enough to drizzle. Drizzle glaze over pie pops; let stand until set, about 30 minutes.

1 Pie Pop: Calories 310; Total Fat 12g (Saturated Fat 5g, Trans Fat 0g); Cholesterol 5mg; Sodium 270mg; Total Carbohydrate 49g (Dietary Fiber 1g); Protein 2g **Exchanges:** ½ Starch, 1 ½ Fruit, 1 Other Carbohydrate, 2½ Fat **Carbohydrate Choices:** 3

tidbit

Make other flavors of pie pops by substituting 1 cup of your favorite canned pie filling for the strawberry-rhubarb filling.

raspberry–white chocolate pie pops

PREP TIME: **20 Minutes** | START TO FINISH: **45 Minutes** | **8 pie pops**

1 box refrigerated pie crusts, softened as directed on box

24 fresh raspberries

8 white candy melts or coating wafers, chopped

8 craft sticks (flat wooden sticks with round ends)

1 egg, beaten

2 tablespoons coarse white sparkling sugar

1 Heat oven to 450°F. Spray cookie sheet with cooking spray.

2 Unroll pie crusts on floured work surface. With 3½-inch round cutter, cut 8 rounds from each crust. Place 8 rounds on cookie sheet. Place 3 raspberries in center of each round; sprinkle chopped candy melts evenly over raspberries.

3 Place 1 craft stick on each round, so tip of stick is in center of round. Top each with 1 remaining round. Press edges together; seal and flute. Cut 4 or 5 small slits in top crust. Brush tops with egg; sprinkle with sugar.

4 Bake 10 to 13 minutes or until golden brown. Remove from cookie sheet to cooling rack; cool 10 minutes before serving.

1 Pie Pop: Calories 150; Total Fat 8g (Saturated Fat 3.5g, Trans Fat 0g); Cholesterol 25mg; Sodium 140mg; Total Carbohydrate 18g (Dietary Fiber 0g); Protein 1g **Exchanges:** ½ Starch, ½ Other Carbohydrate, 1½ Fat **Carbohydrate Choices:** 1

clever cookies, cakes and pies

Have your cake—cookies and pies, too—with these little gems. From cookie bites to baby tarts, these treats are perfect for every occasion!

stout french silk cookie cups

PREP TIME: **30 Minutes** | START TO FINISH: **5 Hours** | **3 dozen cookie cups**

FILLING

- 1 cup whole milk
- ⅓ cup stout beer
- 1 box (4-serving size) chocolate pudding and pie filling mix (not instant)
- ¾ cup semisweet chocolate chips

COOKIE CUPS

- 1 pouch (1 lb 1.5 oz) sugar cookie mix
- ½ cup butter, softened
- 1 egg

TOPPING

- ⅓ cup whipping cream
- 1 tablespoon powdered sugar
- 1 tablespoon stout beer
- ¼ teaspoon vanilla

GARNISH

Chocolate shavings or curls

1 In 2-quart saucepan, cook all filling ingredients except chocolate chips over medium heat 5 to 8 minutes, stirring constantly, until mixture comes to a full boil. Remove from heat. Stir in chocolate chips until melted and smooth. Pour into medium bowl; cover surface of pudding with plastic wrap. Refrigerate about 2 hours or until cold.

2 Meanwhile, heat oven to 375°F. In large bowl, stir cookie cup ingredients until soft dough forms. Shape dough into 36 (1¼-inch) balls (about 1 tablespoon each); place in ungreased mini muffin cups.

3 Bake 9 to 11 minutes or until edges are light golden brown. Immediately press indentation into each with end of wooden spoon. Cool completely in pan, about 30 minutes. Remove from pan to serving plate.

4 Spoon scant 1 tablespoon filling into each cookie cup. Refrigerate at least 2 hours or until set.

5 Just before serving, in chilled medium bowl, beat topping ingredients with electric mixer on high speed until soft peaks form. Spoon about 1 teaspoon topping onto each cup. Garnish each with chocolate shavings. Store covered in refrigerator.

1 Cookie Cup: Calories 130; Total Fat 6g (Saturated Fat 3g, Trans Fat 0.5g); Cholesterol 15mg; Sodium 75mg; Total Carbohydrate 16g (Dietary Fiber 0g); Protein 1g **Exchanges:** ½ Starch, ½ Other Carbohydrate, 1 Fat **Carbohydrate Choices:** 1

tidbit

To make chocolate shavings for a garnish, start with a room-temperature block of chocolate and use a vegetable peeler to shave flat, thin strips from the block of chocolate.

chocolate truffle meringues

PREP TIME: 25 Minutes | **START TO FINISH:** 2 Hours 10 Minutes | **2 dozen cookies**

MERINGUES

- 2 egg whites
- 1/3 cup granulated sugar
- 1/2 cup powdered sugar
- 2 tablespoons unsweetened baking cocoa

FILLING

- 1/4 cup whipping cream
- 3 oz bittersweet baking chocolate, chopped, or 1/2 cup dark chocolate chips
- 2 tablespoons butter, cut into small pieces

tidbits

Cooking parchment paper is a grease- and moisture-resistant paper that prevents baked goods from sticking to pans. It also keeps the pans clean. Look for it near the foil at the grocery store.

Cookies can be made up to 24 hours before serving; store in tightly covered container. Up to 2 hours before serving, spoon in filling and store in refrigerator until ready to serve.

1 Heat oven to 200°F. Line cookie sheet with cooking parchment paper.

2 In medium bowl, beat egg whites with electric mixer on medium speed until soft peaks form. Gradually add granulated sugar, beating on high speed just until stiff peaks form. In small bowl, mix powdered sugar and cocoa. Fold cocoa mixture, 1/3 at a time, into beaten egg whites.

3 Spoon mixture into decorating bag fitted with star tip. Draw 1½-inch-diameter circle on white paper; place under parchment paper as a guide. On parchment paper, pipe mixture into 24 (1½-inch) rounds or spoon into dollops. With back of teaspoon, make an indentation in each to hold filling.

4 Bake 1 to 1¼ hours or until crisp. Cool completely, about 10 minutes.

5 Meanwhile, in 1-quart heavy saucepan, heat whipping cream over medium-low heat just to simmering. Remove from heat; stir in chocolate with whisk until melted. Stir in butter pieces, a few at a time, until melted. Refrigerate until thickened, about 30 minutes.

6 Just before serving, spoon or pipe about 1 teaspoon filling into indentation of each meringue.

1 Cookie: Calories 60 (Calories from Fat 35); Total Fat 35g (Saturated Fat 25g); Cholesterol 5mg; Sodium 15mg; Total Carbohydrate 7g (Dietary Fiber 0g); Protein 0g **Exchanges:** ½ Other Carbohydrate, ½ Fat **Carbohydrate Choices:** ½

mini rainbow whoopie pies

PREP TIME: **2 Hours** | START TO FINISH: **2 Hours** | 50 whoopie pies

COOKIES

- 2 tablespoons butter, softened
- ½ cup granulated sugar
- 1½ cups Original Bisquick mix
- 1 egg
- ⅓ cup milk
- 1 teaspoon vanilla
- Red, yellow, green and blue food colors

FILLING

- 4 oz (half of 8-oz package) cream cheese, softened
- ¼ cup butter, softened
- ½ teaspoon vanilla
- 1¼ cups powdered sugar

tidbits

For larger whoopie pies, use about ½ teaspoon dough per cookie. Bake 6 to 7 minutes.

For a brighter pop of color, use gel food color in place of the liquid.

1 Heat oven to 350°F. Line large cookie sheets with cooking parchment paper.

2 In medium bowl, beat 2 tablespoons butter and the granulated sugar with electric mixer on low speed until well blended and sandy in texture. Add Bisquick mix, egg, milk and vanilla. Beat on medium speed 2 minutes, scraping bowl occasionally, until smooth. Divide batter evenly among 5 small bowls, about ⅓ cup each.

3 Stir food color into each as desired to create rainbow colors. Stir until well blended. Spoon batter into individual resealable food-storage plastic bags. Cut ¼ inch off corner of each bag. Onto cookie sheets, squeeze each bag of colored batter gently to make 20 (½-inch) circles of dough (about ¼ teaspoon each), about 1 inch apart.

4 Bake 3 to 5 minutes or until tops spring back when lightly touched. Cool 2 minutes. Gently remove from cookie sheets to cooling racks; cool completely, about 20 minutes.

5 In medium bowl, beat cream cheese, ¼ cup butter and ½ teaspoon vanilla with electric mixer on low speed until well mixed. Gradually add powdered sugar, beating on low speed until incorporated. Increase speed to medium; beat about 1 minute or until smooth.

6 For each whoopie pie, spread about ½ teaspoon filling on bottom of 1 cookie; place second cookie, bottom side down, on filling. Store loosely covered in refrigerator.

1 Whoopie Pie: Calories 60; Total Fat 2.5g (Saturated Fat 1.5g, Trans Fat 0g); Cholesterol 10mg; Sodium 70mg; Total Carbohydrate 8g (Dietary Fiber 0g); Protein 0g **Exchanges:** ½ Other Carbohydrate, ½ Fat **Carbohydrate Choices:** ½

mini burger cookies

PREP TIME: **40 Minutes** | START TO FINISH: **1 Hour 40 Minutes** | **16 burger cookies**

1 pouch (1 lb 1.5 oz) sugar cookie mix

3 tablespoons all-purpose flour

⅓ cup butter, softened

1 egg

2 tablespoons flaked coconut

Few drops green food color

½ cup vanilla creamy ready-to-spread frosting (from 1-lb container)

16 chocolate-covered peppermint patties (1.5 oz each), unwrapped

1 can (6.4 oz) red decorating icing

1 can (6.4 oz) yellow decorating icing

1 teaspoon honey

1 teaspoon water

2 teaspoons sesame seed

1 Heat oven to 375°F. In medium bowl, stir cookie mix, flour, butter and egg until soft dough forms. Shape dough into 32 (1-inch) balls. On ungreased cookie sheets, place balls 1 inch apart. Bake 10 to 12 minutes or until set and edges are light golden brown. Cool 1 minute; remove to cooling racks. Cool completely.

2 In small resealable food-storage plastic bag, place coconut; add food color. Seal bag; shake until coconut is evenly tinted. Spread slightly less than 1 teaspoon vanilla frosting on bottom of each cookie.

3 For each burger, place 1 peppermint patty on frosted side of 1 cookie. Pipe red and yellow icing on peppermint patty for ketchup and mustard. Top each with about ½ teaspoon green coconut for lettuce. Top with a second cookie, frosting side down; gently press together.

4 In small bowl, mix honey and water. Brush on tops of cookies; sprinkle with sesame seed.

1 Burger Cookie: Calories 480; Total Fat 15g (Saturated Fat 5g, Trans Fat 2g); Cholesterol 25mg; Sodium 230mg; Total Carbohydrate 84g (Dietary Fiber 0g); Protein 2g **Exchanges:** 1 Starch, 4½ Other Carbohydrate, 3 Fat **Carbohydrate Choices:** 5½

chocolate-filled orange-rosemary butter balls

PREP TIME: 1 Hour | **START TO FINISH: 1 Hour 30 Minutes** | **3 dozen sandwich cookies**

COOKIES

- 1 cup butter, softened
- ½ cup powdered sugar
- 1 tablespoon grated orange peel
- 1 tablespoon finely chopped fresh rosemary leaves
- ¼ teaspoon salt
- 1 teaspoon vanilla
- 2 cups all-purpose flour
- ½ teaspoon baking powder
- ¼ cup coarse white decorator sugar crystals, if desired

FILLING

- ½ cup dark chocolate chips
- 2 tablespoons whipping cream

1 Heat oven to 400°F. In large bowl, beat butter, powdered sugar, orange peel, rosemary, salt and vanilla with electric mixer on low speed until mixed; beat on medium speed until creamy. On low speed, beat in flour and baking powder until dough forms.

2 In small bowl, place decorator sugar. Shape dough into 60 (1-inch) balls. Roll in sugar. On ungreased cookie sheets, place balls 2 inches apart. Press lightly with tines of fork to flatten slightly.

3 Bake 6 to 8 minutes or just until edges start to brown. Remove from cookie sheets to cooling racks; cool completely.

4 Meanwhile, in small microwavable bowl, microwave chocolate chips and whipping cream uncovered on High in 15-second intervals until chips can be stirred smooth. Refrigerate until cooled and mixture starts to set, about 10 minutes.

5 For each sandwich cookie, spread about ½ teaspoon filling on bottom of 1 cookie. Press bottom of second cookie over filling. Let stand until set.

1 Sandwich Cookie: Calories 110; Total Fat 7g (Saturated Fat 4.5g, Trans Fat 0g); Cholesterol 20mg; Sodium 75mg; Total Carbohydrate 10g (Dietary Fiber 0g); Protein 1g **Exchanges:** ½ Other Carbohydrate, 1½ Fat **Carbohydrate Choices:** ½

tidbits

Place filled cookies sideways in individual petit four paper cups or mini paper baking cups.

If you bake 2 cookie sheets at a time, switch their positions in the oven halfway through baking.

chocolate-dipped olive sablés

PREP TIME: 45 Minutes | **START TO FINISH: 1 Hour 15 Minutes** | **4 dozen cookies**

COOKIES

- ¾ cup plus 2 tablespoons butter, softened
- ¼ cup sugar
- 2 cups all-purpose flour
- ½ cup finely chopped kalamata olives, drained, patted dry with a paper towel
- ½ cup finely chopped pistachio nuts
- ½ cup finely chopped dark chocolate chips

TOPPING

- 1 cup dark chocolate chips
- 1 teaspoon vegetable oil
- ½ cup finely chopped pistachio nuts

1 Heat oven to 350°F. In large bowl, stir ¾ cup of the butter and the sugar until well mixed. Stir in flour (if dough is crumbly, mix in up to 2 additional tablespoons softened butter). Stir in remaining cookie ingredients.

2 On work surface lightly sprinkled with flour, roll dough ¼ inch thick. Cut with 2-inch round cutter. On ungreased cookie sheets, place rounds ½ inch apart.

3 Bake 15 to 18 minutes or until set. Immediately remove from cookie sheets to cooling racks.

4 In small microwavable bowl, microwave 1 cup chocolate chips and the oil uncovered on High 1 minute 30 seconds, stirring every 30 seconds or until mixture can be stirred smooth. Dip half of each cookie into chocolate; wipe excess on edge of bowl. Sprinkle edge of dipped half with finely chopped pistachio nuts. Place on waxed paper to set, about 1 hour.

1 Cookie: Calories 100; Total Fat 6g (Saturated Fat 3.5g, Trans Fat 0g); Cholesterol 10mg; Sodium 40mg; Total Carbohydrate 9g (Dietary Fiber 0g); Protein 1g **Exchanges:** ½ Starch, 1 Fat **Carbohydrate Choices:** ½

tidbit

Dipping the cookie in chocolate gives it a finished look, but if you're short on time, simply drizzle the melted chocolate over the cooled cookies.

mini holiday confetti cookies

PREP TIME: 20 Minutes | **START TO FINISH:** 2 Hours 30 Minutes | 50 servings (4 cookies each)

1 pouch (1 lb 1.5 oz) sugar cookie mix

⅓ cup butter, melted

1 egg

2 tablespoons all-purpose flour

3 containers (2 oz each) multicolored candy sprinkles

1 In medium bowl, stir cookie mix, melted butter, egg and flour until soft dough forms.

2 Divide dough into eight even sections. Shape each into a roll, 8 inches long and ½ inch in diameter. Roll in candy sprinkles. Wrap and refrigerate at least 2 hours, until firm.

3 Heat oven to 350°F. Cut each roll into 24 (¼-inch) slices. Place ½ inch apart on ungreased cookie sheets.

4 Bake 5 to 7 minutes or until light brown. Cool 1 minute; remove from cookie sheets to cooling racks.

1 Serving: Calories 150; Total Fat 7g (Saturated Fat 4g, Trans Fat 1g); Cholesterol 15mg; Sodium 80mg; Total Carbohydrate 22g (Dietary Fiber 0g); Protein 1g **Exchanges:** ½ Starch, 1 Other Carbohydrate, 1½ Fat **Carbohydrate Choices:** 1½

tidbit

To easily roll the dough in sprinkles, place a sheet of plastic wrap on a cookie sheet or tray with sides. Place roll in plastic wrap, and pour 3 tablespoons sprinkles over dough. Move roll of dough back and forth, using plastic to press sprinkles onto sides of dough, until sides are completely coated. Wrap in plastic wrap and refrigerate.

mini cookie collection

PREP TIME: **1 Hour 30 Minutes** | START TO FINISH: **1 Hour 30 Minutes** | **9½ dozen cookies**

1 pouch (1 lb 1.5 oz) chocolate chip, peanut butter or sugar cookie mix

Ingredients called for on cookie mix pouch

Sugar, if needed

Cinnamon, if needed

108 (about 1 cup) miniature semisweet or milk chocolate candy drops for baking (from 10-oz bag), if needed

1 Heat oven to 350°F. Make cookie dough as directed on pouch.

2 Shape dough as desired following ideas below.

3 Bake 8 to 10 minutes or until edges are light golden brown.

mini chocolate chippers: Make chocolate chip cookie mix as directed. Drop dough by rounded ½ teaspoonfuls 1 inch apart on ungreased cookie sheet. Bake as directed above. Cool 1 minute before removing from cookie sheet.

mini peanut blossom cookies: Make peanut butter cookie mix as directed. Shape dough into ½-inch balls; roll in sugar. Place balls 1 inch apart on ungreased cookie sheet. Bake as directed above. Immediately press miniature chocolate candy drop in top of each cookie. Cool 1 minute before removing from cookie sheet.

snicker-do-littles: Make sugar cookie mix as directed. Shape dough into ½-inch balls. Mix 3 tablespoons sugar and 1 teaspoon cinnamon. Roll dough balls in sugar mixture. Place on ungreased cookie sheet. Bake as directed above. Cool 1 minute before removing from cookie sheet.

1 Cookie: Calories 35; Total Fat 2g (Saturated Fat 1g, Trans Fat 0g); Cholesterol 0mg; Sodium 20mg; Total Carbohydrate 4g (Dietary Fiber 0g); Protein 0g **Exchanges:** ½ Fat **Carbohydrate Choices:** 0

tidbits

Keep a stash of mini cookies in the freezer for up to 2 months. They thaw quickly and will be ready when you need them.

Mini cookies are great for kids' snacks. Pack them in mini snack bags for lunches or snacks.

cupcake poppers

PREP TIME: 1 Hour 15 Minutes | **START TO FINISH:** 1 Hour 15 Minutes | 30 cupcake poppers

CUPCAKES

1 box white cake mix with pudding

Water, vegetable oil and egg whites called for on cake mix box

¼ teaspoon each gel food colors (neon pink, neon purple, neon orange, neon green, classic blue)

FROSTING

1½ cups marshmallow creme

¾ cup butter, softened

1¼ cups powdered sugar

Gel food colors (neon pink, neon purple, neon orange, neon green, classic blue)

1 Heat oven to 350°F. Spray 60 mini muffin cups with cooking spray. Make cake batter as directed on box. Divide batter among 5 small bowls, about ¾ cup each. Make 5 different colors of batter by adding ¼ teaspoon food color to each bowl; blend well.

2 Fill each muffin cup with 1 level measuring tablespoon batter, making 12 cupcakes of each color.

3 Bake 11 to 14 minutes or until toothpick inserted in center comes out clean. Cool 5 minutes; remove from pan to cooling rack. Cool completely, about 10 minutes.

4 In large bowl, beat marshmallow creme and butter with electric mixer on medium speed until blended. Beat in powdered sugar until fluffy. Divide frosting among 5 small bowls, about ⅓ cup each. Using the same 5 food colors, lightly tint frosting in each bowl to match cupcake colors.

5 Assemble each popper using 2 mini cupcakes. Cut tops off each cupcake horizontally (save bottoms for another use). Spread or pipe about 1 tablespoon frosting on cut side of 1 cupcake top. Form a sandwich by placing cut side of second cupcake top on frosting; press lightly. Repeat with remaining cupcake tops. Store loosely covered.

1 Cupcake Popper: Calories 160; Total Fat 8g (Saturated Fat 3.5g, Trans Fat 0g); Cholesterol 10mg; Sodium 150mg; Total Carbohydrate 21g (Dietary Fiber 0g); Protein 1g **Exchanges:** ½ Starch, 1 Other Carbohydrate, 1½ Fat **Carbohydrate Choices:** 1½

tidbit

If you have only one pan and a recipe calls for more cupcakes than your pan will make, cover and refrigerate the rest of the batter while baking the first batch. Cool the pan about 15 minutes, then bake the rest of the batter, adding 1 to 2 minutes to the bake time.

cupcake sliders

PREP TIME: **1 Hour 40 Minutes** | START TO FINISH: **3 Hours 20 Minutes** | **64 cupcake sliders**

CUPCAKES

2⅓ cups all-purpose flour

2½ teaspoons baking powder

½ teaspoon salt

1 cup butter, softened

1¼ cups sugar

3 eggs

1 teaspoon vanilla

⅔ cup milk

BROWNIES

1 box fudge brownie mix

¼ cup water

⅔ cup vegetable oil

2 eggs

TOPPINGS

1½ cups flaked coconut

4 to 6 drops green food color

4 to 6 drops water

1 cup chocolate creamy ready-to-spread frosting (from 1-lb container)

64 orange juicy chewy fruit candies, unwrapped

16 rolls strawberry chewy fruit snack (from three 4.5-oz boxes), unwrapped

2 tablespoons honey

1 to 2 teaspoons water

2 tablespoons sesame seed

1 Heat oven to 350°F. Place mini paper baking cup in each of 24 mini muffin cups. In medium bowl, mix flour, baking powder and salt; set aside. In large bowl, beat butter with electric mixer on medium speed 30 seconds. Gradually add sugar, about ¼ cup at a time, beating well after each addition. Beat 2 minutes longer. Add 3 eggs, one at a time, beating well after each addition. Beat in vanilla. On low speed, alternately add flour mixture, about a third at a time, and milk, about half at a time, beating just until blended.

2 Fill each cup with about 1 tablespoon plus 1 teaspoon batter or until about two-thirds full. (Cover and refrigerate remaining batter until ready to bake; cool pan 15 minutes before reusing.) Bake 17 to 20 minutes or until golden brown and toothpick inserted in center comes out clean. Cool 5 minutes; remove cupcakes from pans to cooling racks. Cool completely, about 15 minutes. Repeat with remaining batter to make an additional 48 mini cupcakes.

3 Leave oven temperature at 350°F. Grease 15x10x1-inch pan with shortening or cooking spray. In large bowl, stir brownie mix, ¼ cup water, the oil and 2 eggs with spoon until blended. Pour into pan. Bake 22 to 26 minutes or until toothpick inserted 2 inches from side of pan comes out almost clean. Cool 20 minutes. With 1½-inch round cutter, cut 64 brownie rounds for "burgers."

4 In medium bowl, toss coconut, green food color and 4 to 6 drops water with fork until coconut reaches desired color; set aside. Remove paper baking cups from 64 cupcakes (reserve remaining cupcakes for another use). Cut each cupcake horizontally in half to make tops and bottoms of "buns." Place brownie rounds (burgers) on bottom halves of cupcakes (buns), using frosting to secure.

5 To make "cheese slices," on large microwavable plate, microwave about 8 chewy fruit candies at a time on High 5 to 10

seconds to soften. Use bottom of measuring cup to flatten until each is about 1¾ inches in diameter. Secure to "burgers" with frosting. Repeat to make additional "cheese slices."

6 To make "ketchup," cut chewy fruit snack with kitchen scissors into about 1¾-inch irregular-edged circles. Secure to "cheese" with frosting. Spread dab of frosting on "ketchup"; sprinkle each slider with scant 2 teaspoons tinted coconut for "shredded lettuce."

7 In small bowl, mix honey and enough of the 1 to 2 teaspoons water until thin consistency. Brush honey mixture lightly over "bun tops"; sprinkle each with sesame seed. Spread dab of frosting on cut sides of "bun tops"; secure to coconut, frosting side down.

1 Cupcake Slider: Calories 190; Total Fat 8g (Saturated Fat 3.5g, Trans Fat 0g); Cholesterol 25mg; Sodium 135mg; Total Carbohydrate 27g (Dietary Fiber 0g); Protein 1g **Exchanges:** ½ Starch, 1½ Other Carbohydrate, 1½ Fat **Carbohydrate Choices:** 2

tidbits

Brownies can be baked ahead, but wait to cut out the "burgers" until ready to assemble so the burgers don't dry out.

For a fun touch, serve these "sliders" in red and white checked paper food trays, like at a fast-food restaurant, accompanied by "fries" (yellow licorice twists).

chipotle devil's food mini cupcakes

PREP TIME: **35 Minutes** | START TO FINISH: **1 Hour 15 Minutes** | **32 mini cupcakes**

CUPCAKES

1	cup all-purpose flour
¾	cup granulated sugar
⅓	cup unsweetened dark baking cocoa
½	teaspoon baking soda
½	teaspoon salt
½	teaspoon ground cinnamon
¼	teaspoon chipotle chili powder
½	cup buttermilk
⅓	cup butter, softened
½	teaspoon vanilla
1	egg

FROSTING

6	oz cream cheese, softened
3	cups powdered sugar
½	to 1 teaspoon milk
	Red gel or paste food color
	Green food color

1 Heat oven to 350°F. Place mini paper baking cup in each of 32 mini muffin cups. In large bowl, beat cupcake ingredients with electric mixer on low speed until moistened, then on medium speed 2 minutes. Fill muffin cups two-thirds to three-fourths full, about 1 tablespoon per cup.

2 Bake 15 to 18 minutes or until toothpick inserted in center comes out clean. Let stand 10 minutes; remove from pans to cooling racks. Cool completely, about 20 minutes.

3 In small bowl, beat cream cheese and powdered sugar with electric mixer on low speed until mixed, then at medium speed until creamy. Spoon 2 tablespoons into one custard cup and 2 tablespoons into another custard cup; set aside. To remaining frosting, gradually beat in enough milk to make frosting smooth and spreadable. Frost cupcakes.

4 Stir small amount of red food color into 2 tablespoons of the frosting, or until bright red. Stir 1 drop green food color into remaining 2 tablespoons frosting or until medium green. Spoon each colored frosting into small resealable food-storage plastic bag. Cut ¼-inch opening in one corner of red frosting bag. Pipe small chili pepper shape on top of each cupcake, curving slightly and tapering to a soft point. Cut tiny opening in one corner of green frosting bag. Squiggle a little frosting at wide end of pepper for stem. Store in refrigerator.

1 Mini Cupcake: Calories 120; Total Fat 4g (Saturated Fat 2.5g, Trans Fat 0g); Cholesterol 15mg; Sodium 95mg; Total Carbohydrate 20g (Dietary Fiber 0g); Protein 1g **Exchanges:** ½ Starch, 1 Other Carbohydrate, ½ Fat **Carbohydrate Choices:** 1

tidbits

The chipotle chili powder gives these chocolaty treats a slightly smoky flavor plus a bit of heat. You can use regular chili powder, which will provide less heat, or ancho chili powder, which will provide some heat but no smoky flavor. Look for the specialty chili powders with the other spices at the supermarket.

Gel or paste food color will provide a vibrant red color without softening the frosting. You can use liquid food color, but the frosting might not hold its shape as well.

orange-thyme mini cupcakes

PREP TIME: 25 Minutes | **START TO FINISH:** 50 Minutes | **24 mini cupcakes**

CAKE

¾	cup all-purpose flour
1	teaspoon baking soda
⅛	teaspoon salt
⅓	cup granulated sugar
¼	cup butter, softened
1	egg plus 1 egg white
2	tablespoons milk
2	teaspoons grated orange peel
1½	teaspoons chopped fresh thyme leaves

GARNISH

1	tablespoon granulated sugar
2	teaspoons grated orange peel

GLAZE

1	cup powdered sugar
4	to 6 teaspoons orange juice

1 Heat oven to 350°F. Grease 24 mini muffin cups with shortening, or spray with cooking spray.

2 In small bowl, mix flour, baking soda and salt; set aside. In medium bowl, beat ⅓ cup granulated sugar and butter with electric mixer on medium speed until creamy. Add egg and egg white, milk, 2 teaspoons orange peel and the thyme; beat on medium speed 1 minute, scraping bowl occasionally. On low speed, beat in flour mixture, just until blended. Fill muffin cups about two-thirds full.

3 Bake 9 to 12 minutes or until toothpick inserted in center comes out clean. Cool in pan 5 minutes; remove cupcakes to cooling racks. Cool completely, about 20 minutes.

4 In small bowl, combine 1 tablespoon granulated sugar and 2 teaspoons orange peel; set aside. In another small bowl, mix powdered sugar and enough orange juice for drizzling consistency. Using fork or spoon, drizzle glaze over tops of cupcakes. Sprinkle with orange peel mixture. To serve, place cupcakes in mini paper baking cups.

1 Mini Cupcake: Calories 70; Total Fat 2g (Saturated Fat 1.5g, Trans Fat 0g); Cholesterol 15mg; Sodium 85mg; Total Carbohydrate 12g (Dietary Fiber 0g); Protein 1g **Exchanges:** ½ Starch, ½ Fat **Carbohydrate Choices:** 1

tidbit

Wait a minute—thyme in a little cake? Adding savory flavors to typically sweet items is a growing trend. Try these tasty little cakes; we think you'll like them.

mini red velvet cheesecakes

PREP TIME: 20 Minutes | **START TO FINISH:** 3 Hours | **16 servings**

24 thin chocolate wafer cookies, crushed (1¼ cups)

3 tablespoons butter, melted

2 packages (8 oz each) plus 4 oz cream cheese, softened

1 cup granulated sugar

¼ cup unsweetened baking cocoa

2 teaspoons vanilla

2 tablespoons red food color

3 eggs

½ cup whipping cream

1 tablespoon granulated or powdered sugar

Chocolate curls, if desired

1 Heat oven to 350°F. Place foil baking cup in each of 16 regular-size muffin cups. Mix cookie crumbs and butter. Firmly press mixture in bottoms of baking cups with back of spoon. In medium bowl, beat cream cheese with electric mixer on medium speed until smooth. Gradually beat in 1 cup granulated sugar and the cocoa until fluffy. Beat in vanilla and food color. Beat in eggs, one at a time, until well blended. Divide batter evenly among baking cups (cups will be almost full).

2 Bake 20 to 25 minutes or until centers are firm. Cool 15 minutes (centers will sink). Remove from pans. Refrigerate at least 1 hour. Cover; refrigerate at least 1 hour longer.

3 In chilled small bowl, beat whipping cream and 1 tablespoon sugar with electric mixer on high speed until stiff. Just before serving, peel off baking cups. Top cheesecakes with whipped cream and chocolate curls. Store in refrigerator.

1 Serving: Calories 290; Total Fat 19g (Saturated Fat 11g, Trans Fat 0.5g); Cholesterol 95mg; Sodium 210mg; Total Carbohydrate 23g (Dietary Fiber 0g); Protein 4g **Exchanges:** ½ Starch, ½ Other Carbohydrate, ½ Milk, 3 Fat **Carbohydrate Choices:** 1½

tidbits

Cheesecake freezes beautifully! Wrap tightly, and freeze up to 5 months. Thaw in the original wrapping in the refrigerator 2 to 4 hours.

To make chocolate curls, place a bar or block of chocolate on waxed paper. Make curls by pressing firmly against the chocolate and pulling a vegetable peeler toward you in long, thin strokes. Small curls can be made by using the side of the chocolate bar. Transfer each curl carefully with a toothpick to a waxed paper–lined cookie sheet or directly onto cheesecake.

cookies and cream mini cheesecakes

PREP TIME: **25 Minutes** | START TO FINISH: **2 Hours 10 Minutes** | **24 servings**

16	creme-filled chocolate sandwich cookies, crushed (about 1½ cups)
2	tablespoons butter, melted
1	package (8 oz) cream cheese, softened
¼	cup milk
2	tablespoons sugar
1	teaspoon vanilla
1	egg
4	creme-filled chocolate sandwich cookies, cut into ¼-inch pieces (about ½ cup)
3	tablespoons semisweet chocolate chips
1	teaspoon shortening

1 Heat oven to 325°F. Line 24 miniature muffin cups with paper baking cups. In small bowl, mix crushed cookies and melted butter. Press 1 teaspoon cookie mixture firmly in bottom of each muffin cup.

2 In large bowl, beat cream cheese, milk and sugar with electric mixer on medium speed until light and fluffy. Add vanilla and egg; beat well. Fold in cut-up cookies. Spoon 1 heaping tablespoon cream cheese mixture into each crust-lined muffin cup.

3 Bake 12 to 14 minutes or until edges are set and centers are still soft. Cool in pan on cooling rack 30 minutes. Refrigerate at least 1 hour or up to 48 hours before serving.

4 Just before serving, in 1-cup microwavable measuring cup, microwave chocolate chips and shortening uncovered on High 30 to 45 seconds or until melted, stirring once. Drizzle chocolate over tops of cheesecakes. Store in refrigerator.

1 Serving: Calories 100; Total Fat 6g (Saturated Fat 3.5g, Trans Fat 0.5g); Cholesterol 20mg; Sodium 95mg; Total Carbohydrate 8g (Dietary Fiber 0g); Protein 2g **Exchanges:** ½ Starch, 1½ Fat **Carbohydrate Choices:** ½

tidbits

To reduce the fat in each cheesecake by about 3 grams, use fat-free cream cheese.

These mini cheesecakes can be made and frozen up to a month ahead.

chocolate-cherry mini lava cakes

PREP TIME: **20 Minutes** | START TO FINISH: **45 Minutes** | **12 servings**

CAKES

- 1 teaspoon shortening
- 2 tablespoons plus 2 teaspoons unsweetened baking cocoa
- ½ cup plus 1 teaspoon all-purpose flour
- ½ cup semisweet chocolate chips
- 1 tablespoon vegetable oil
- 1 cup powdered sugar
- ½ cup fat-free egg product
- 1 container (5.3 oz) black cherry fat-free Greek yogurt

TOPPINGS, IF DESIRED

- 1 tablespoon powdered sugar
- 12 cherries, with stems

1 Heat oven to 350°F. Lightly grease 12 regular-size muffin cups with shortening. In small bowl, stir together 2 teaspoons of the baking cocoa and 1 teaspoon of the flour; lightly sprinkle in muffin cups.

2 In medium bowl, microwave chocolate chips and oil uncovered on High 1 to 2 minutes, stirring every 30 seconds, until mixture is melted and smooth. Stir in 1 cup powdered sugar and the egg product with whisk until blended. Stir in 2 tablespoons baking cocoa, the yogurt and ½ cup flour. Spoon batter evenly into muffin cups, filling each about two-thirds full.

3 Bake 9 to 10 minutes, or until sides are firm (centers will still be soft). Let stand 2 minutes. Place serving platter upside down on muffin pan. Turn platter and muffin pan over; remove muffin pan. Sprinkle cakes with powdered sugar, and top each with a cherry. Serve immediately.

1 Serving: Calories 130; Total Fat 4g (Saturated Fat 1.5g, Trans Fat 0g); Cholesterol 0mg; Sodium 25mg; Total Carbohydrate 20g (Dietary Fiber 1g); Protein 3g **Exchanges:** 1 Starch, ½ Other Carbohydrate, ½ Fat **Carbohydrate Choices:** 1

impossibly easy
mini pumpkin pies

PREP TIME: 10 Minutes | **START TO FINISH: 1 Hour** | **12 servings**

1   cup canned pumpkin
(not pumpkin pie mix)

½   cup Original Bisquick mix

½   cup sugar

¾   cup evaporated milk

1½ teaspoons pumpkin pie spice

1   teaspoon vanilla

2   eggs

1   cup frozen (thawed) whipped
topping, if desired

1 Heat oven to 375°F. Spray 12 regular-size muffin cups with cooking spray.

2 In medium bowl, stir all ingredients except whipped topping until blended. Spoon ¼ cup of mixture into each muffin cup.

3 Bake about 30 minutes or until muffin tops are golden brown and edges start to pull away from sides of cups. Cool 10 minutes. Run knife around sides of cups to loosen pies; remove from pan to cooling rack. Cool 10 minutes longer; serve with whipped topping. Store in refrigerator.

1 Serving: Calories 90; Total Fat 2g (Saturated Fat 1g, Trans Fat 0g); Cholesterol 35mg; Sodium 90mg; Total Carbohydrate 15g (Dietary Fiber 0g); Protein 2g **Exchanges:** ½ Starch, ½ Other Carbohydrate, ½ Fat **Carbohydrate Choices:** 1

gingery lemon curd petite pies

PREP TIME: 40 Minutes | **START TO FINISH: 1 Hour 10 Minutes** | **16 servings**

LEMON CURD

- ½ cup granulated sugar
- 1 tablespoon cornstarch
- 2 teaspoons grated lemon peel
- ½ cup fresh lemon juice
- 2 eggs, slightly beaten
- 1 tablespoon finely chopped crystallized ginger

CRUST

- 1 box refrigerated pie crusts, softened as directed on box

GARNISH

Powdered sugar

1 In 1-quart saucepan, mix granulated sugar and cornstarch. Stir in lemon peel, lemon juice, eggs and ginger with whisk until blended. Cook over medium heat about 2 minutes, stirring constantly, until mixture thickens and boils. Remove from heat; transfer to bowl. Cover with plastic wrap; refrigerate about 30 minutes or until completely cool.

2 Meanwhile, heat oven to 375°F. Line 2 cookie sheets with cooking parchment paper. On lightly floured surface, roll 1 pie crust ⅛ inch thick. With 3-inch round cutter, cut out 16 rounds (you may need to reroll scraps to get 16 rounds). Place on cookie sheet. With fork, poke holes all over rounds. Repeat with second pie crust, except don't poke with fork. With 1½-inch fluted cookie cutter, cut out center of second batch of rounds. Place on cookie sheet.

3 Bake 8 to 10 minutes or until golden brown. Remove from cookie sheets to cooling racks; cool completely.

4 To serve, place 1 plain pastry round in each of 16 jumbo paper baking cups. Top each with about 1 tablespoon lemon curd. Sprinkle powdered sugar over rounds with fluted cutouts; place 1 round over lemon curd in each cup.

1 Serving: Calories 180; Total Fat 9g (Saturated Fat 2.5g, Trans Fat 0g); Cholesterol 25mg; Sodium 160mg; Total Carbohydrate 21g (Dietary Fiber 0g); Protein 2g **Exchanges:** 1 Starch, ½ Other Carbohydrate, 1½ Fat **Carbohydrate Choices:** 1½

tidbit

For a more decorative look, use heart-shaped cookie cutters.

cherry-filled heart-shaped pies

PREP TIME: **45 Minutes** | START TO FINISH: **2 Hours 45 Minutes** | **6 servings**

FILLING

- ⅔ cup granulated sugar
- 2 tablespoons cornstarch
- 1 can (15 oz) pitted dark sweet cherries, drained, 3 tablespoons juice reserved
- 1 teaspoon grated orange peel
- ½ cup orange juice
- 1 tablespoon unsalted butter
- 1 vanilla bean

CRUST

- 1 box refrigerated pie crusts, softened as directed on box

TOPPING

- 1 egg
- 1 tablespoon whipping cream
- 2 tablespoons coarse sugar or sanding sugar

1 In 2-quart saucepan, mix granulated sugar and cornstarch with whisk. Stir in cherries, reserved juice, the orange peel, orange juice and butter. Cut slit down center of vanilla bean; scrape out seeds. Add seeds and bean to cherry mixture. Heat to boiling; boil 1 minute, stirring constantly. Pour into shallow container. Remove and discard vanilla bean. Refrigerate until ready to assemble.

2 Meanwhile, on lightly floured surface, roll 1 pie crust ⅛ inch thick. With 5½-inch heart-shaped cookie cutter, cut out 6 hearts. Place on cookie sheet. Repeat with second pie crust. With 1½-inch heart-shaped cookie cutter, cut out small heart from center of second batch of hearts. Spread 2 tablespoons filling on each plain heart. Cover with cutout hearts so filling shows. Press edges together with fork. Refrigerate about 1 hour or until firm.

3 Heat oven to 400°F. In small bowl, beat egg and whipping cream. Brush over hearts. Sprinkle with coarse sugar.

4 Bake 25 to 30 minutes or until lightly golden. Remove from cookie sheet to cooling rack; cool at least 30 minutes before serving.

1 Serving: Calories 570; Total Fat 27g (Saturated Fat 8g, Trans Fat 0g); Cholesterol 40mg; Sodium 410mg; Total Carbohydrate 75g (Dietary Fiber 2g); Protein 6g **Exchanges:** 2 Starch, 1 Fruit, 2 Other Carbohydrate, 5 Fat **Carbohydrate Choices:** 5

tidbits

Sprinkle the pies with powdered sugar after baking for a different look.

If a vanilla bean is not available, substitute ½ to 1 teaspoon pure vanilla.

mini s'mores hand pies

PREP TIME: **35 Minutes** | START TO FINISH: **50 Minutes** | **10 servings**

CRUST

- 1 box refrigerated pie crusts, softened as directed on box
- ½ cup graham cracker crumbs
- ¼ cup sugar
- 3 tablespoons butter, melted

FILLING

- ½ cup marshmallow creme
- 2 tablespoons cream cheese, softened
- 2 tablespoons sugar
- ½ cup semisweet or milk chocolate chips

1 Heat oven to 425°F. Line cookie sheet with cooking parchment paper.

2 Unroll pie crusts on work surface. With 3-inch round cutter, cut 10 rounds from each crust. In shallow bowl, mix cracker crumbs and ¼ cup sugar. Brush both sides of pie crust rounds with butter; dip into crumb mixture to coat.

3 In small bowl, stir together filling ingredients. Spoon about 1 heaping tablespoon filling in center of 10 coated rounds. Top with remaining 10 rounds; pinch edges to seal. Place on cookie sheet.

4 Bake 9 to 12 minutes or until golden brown. Serve warm or cool. Store any remaining pies covered in refrigerator.

1 Serving: Calories 320; Total Fat 17g (Saturated Fat 8g, Trans Fat 0g); Cholesterol 20mg; Sodium 280mg; Total Carbohydrate 39g (Dietary Fiber 0g); Protein 2g **Exchanges:** 1½ Starch, 1 Other Carbohydrate, 3 Fat **Carbohydrate Choices:** 2½

tidbit

For the cream cheese, use 1 oz from a 3 oz package, or scoop out 2 tablespoons from an 8 oz container of cream cheese spread.

tiramisu bites

PREP TIME: 1 Hour | **START TO FINISH: 5 Hours** | **24 servings**

12   slices (¼ inch thick) frozen (thawed) pound cake (from 10-oz package)

¼   cup water

1½   teaspoons instant coffee granules

1½   teaspoons rum extract

1   container (8 oz) mascarpone cheese

¼   cup powdered sugar

½   cup whipping cream

½   oz semisweet baking chocolate

24   espresso coffee beans, if desired

1 Line 24 mini muffin cups with petit four paper cups. Cut 2 (1¼-inch) rounds from each cake slice. Place 1 cake round in bottom of each cup.

2 In small bowl, mix water, coffee granules and ½ teaspoon of the rum extract. Drizzle about ½ teaspoon of the coffee mixture over cake in each muffin cup. Set aside.

3 In medium bowl, beat cheese, powdered sugar and remaining 1 teaspoon rum extract with electric mixer on medium speed until creamy. In another medium bowl, beat whipping cream on high speed until soft peaks form. On low speed, beat cheese mixture into whipped cream. Spoon or pipe 1 rounded tablespoon whipped cream mixture into each cup, covering cake.

4 Grate semisweet chocolate over each cup. Top each with coffee bean. Refrigerate at least 4 hours to blend flavors. Store covered in refrigerator.

1 Serving: Calories 110; Total Fat 8g (Saturated Fat 45g, Trans Fat 0g); Cholesterol 25mg; Sodium 15mg; Total Carbohydrate 9g (Dietary Fiber 0g); Protein 1g **Exchanges:** ½ Starch, 1½ Fat **Carbohydrate Choices:** ½

tidbits

Although these delicious little bites are ready to serve in 5 hours, the flavor and texture actually improve with longer standing. Make a day ahead, and let them mellow in the refrigerator.

Garnish with chocolate-covered espresso coffee beans.

cranberry mousse mini tarts

PREP TIME: **45 Minutes** | START TO FINISH: **2 Hours 5 Minutes** | **24 tarts**

FILLING

- 1 envelope unflavored gelatin
- ²/₃ cup water
- ½ cup granulated sugar
- 1 cup whole cranberries, chopped
- ½ teaspoon grated orange peel

CRUST

- 1 box refrigerated pie crusts, softened as directed on box

  Coarse sugar, if desired

TOPPING

- ¼ cup whipping cream
- 3 teaspoons powdered sugar

tidbit

These mini tarts are the perfect dessert for a holiday party. Both the tarts and the stars can be made a day ahead of time. Store the tarts in the refrigerator and the stars at room temperature. Just before serving, top each tart with a star and a sprinkle of powdered sugar.

1 In small bowl, sprinkle gelatin on water to soften; let stand about 15 minutes. In 1½-quart saucepan, heat ½ cup granulated sugar and the cranberries just to boiling over medium heat, stirring occasionally. Remove from heat; stir in gelatin mixture and orange peel. Refrigerate 30 to 40 minutes or until mixture just starts to thicken.

2 Heat oven to 425°F. Spray 24 miniature muffin cups with cooking spray.

3 Unroll pie crusts on work surface. With 2½-inch scalloped round cutter, cut 15 rounds from first crust and 9 from second crust. Fit rounds into muffin cups, pressing in gently. Generously prick crusts with fork. With 1-inch star-shaped cookie cutter, cut 24 stars from remaining crust; place on ungreased cookie sheet. Sprinkle with coarse sugar.

4 Bake crusts 6 to 9 minutes or until light golden brown. Cool completely on cooling rack, about 15 minutes; remove from muffin cups. Meanwhile, bake star shapes 3 to 4 minutes or until light golden brown.

5 In small bowl, beat whipping cream until soft peaks form. Add 2 teaspoons of the powdered sugar; beat until stiff peaks form. Fold in cranberry mixture; refrigerate about 10 minutes or until thickened. Spoon about 1 tablespoon filling into each tart shell; top each with 1 star. Store in refrigerator. Just before serving, sprinkle with remaining 1 teaspoon powdered sugar.

1 Tart: Calories 80; Total Fat 3.5g (Saturated Fat 1.5g, Trans Fat 0g); Cholesterol 0mg; Sodium 45mg; Total Carbohydrate 10g (Dietary Fiber 0g); Protein 0g **Exchanges:** ½ Other Carbohydrate, 1 Fat **Carbohydrate Choices:** ½

Metric Conversion Guide

Note: The recipes in this cookbook have not been developed or tested using metric measures.
When converting recipes to metric, some variations in quality may be noted.

Volume

U.S. Units	Canadian Metric	Australian Metric
¼ teaspoon	1 mL	1 ml
½ teaspoon	2 mL	2 ml
1 teaspoon	5 mL	5 ml
1 tablespoon	15 mL	20 ml
¼ cup	50 mL	60 ml
⅓ cup	75 mL	80 ml
½ cup	125 mL	125 ml
⅔ cup	150 mL	170 ml
¾ cup	175 mL	190 ml
1 cup	250 mL	250 ml
1 quart	1 liter	1 liter
1½ quarts	1.5 liters	1.5 liters
2 quarts	2 liters	2 liters
2½ quarts	2.5 liters	2.5 liters
3 quarts	3 liters	3 liters
4 quarts	4 liters	4 liters

Weight

U.S. Units	Canadian Metric	Australian Metric
1 ounce	30 grams	30 grams
2 ounces	55 grams	60 grams
3 ounces	85 grams	90 grams
4 ounces (¼ pound)	115 grams	125 grams
8 ounces (½ pound)	225 grams	225 grams
16 ounces (1 pound)	455 grams	500 grams
1 pound	455 grams	0.5 kilogram

Measurements

Inches	Centimeters
1	2.5
2	5.0
3	7.5
4	10.0
5	12.5
6	15.0
7	17.5
8	20.5
9	23.0
10	25.5
11	28.0
12	30.5
13	33.0

Temperatures

Fahrenheit	Celsius
32°	0°
212°	100°
250°	120°
275°	140°
300°	150°
325°	160°
350°	180°
375°	190°
400°	200°
425°	220°
450°	230°
475°	240°
500°	260°

Index

Page numbers in *italics* indicate illustrations

Recipe Testing and Calculating Nutrition Information

Recipe Testing:

- Large eggs and 2% milk were used unless otherwise indicated.

- Fat-free, low-fat, low-sodium or lite products were not used unless indicated.

- No nonstick cookware and bakeware were used unless otherwise indicated. No dark-colored, black or insulated bakeware was used.

- When a pan is specified, a metal pan was used; a baking dish or pie plate means ovenproof glass was used.

- An electric hand mixer was used for mixing only when mixer speeds are specified.

Calculating Nutrition:

- The first ingredient was used wherever a choice is given, such as ½ cup sour cream or plain yogurt.

- The first amount was used wherever a range is given, such as 3- to 3½-pound whole chicken.

- The first serving number was used wherever a range is given, such as 4 to 6 servings.

- "If desired" ingredients were not included.

- Only the amount of a marinade or frying oil that is absorbed was included.